A NATURE GUIDE TO THE
BUTTERFLIES
OF
HONG KONG

Jason Mann

JOHN BEAUFOY PUBLISHING

Dedicated to Hong Kong locals and visitors alike, who might connect with a passing butterfly and discover one more reason to celebrate and care for this great city. To our collective grandchildren, from whom we borrow the present. May they have even more access to healthy air, water and butterflies than we do. And most of all to my dear Natalie, mariposa.

First published in the United Kingdom in 2024 by John Beaufoy Publishing Ltd
11 Blenheim Court, 316 Woodstock Road, Oxford OX2 7NS, England
www.johnbeaufoy.com

Copyright © 2024 John Beaufoy Publishing Limited
Copyright in text © 2024 Jason Mann
Copyright in photographs © see p. 171
Copyright in maps © 2024 John Beaufoy Publishing Limited

Photo Credits
Front cover: *main image* Common Mime Swallowtail (© Stephen Ng); *bottom left* Purple Sapphire (© Crystal Lam), *bottom centre* Fluffy Tit (© Crystal Lam), *bottom right* Monastyrski's Ace (© W. K. Cheng)
Back cover: Peacock Royal (© Tree Fong)
Title page: Jewelled Grass-blue (© Stephen Ng)
Contents page: Chocolate Royal (© Stephen Ng)

All rights reserved. No part of this publication may be reproduced, stored in a retrieval system or transmitted in any form or by any means, electronic, mechanical, photocopying, recording or otherwise, without the prior written permission of the publishers.

Great care has been taken to maintain the accuracy of the information contained in this work. However, neither the publishers nor the authors can be held responsible for any consequences arising from the use of the information contained therein.

ISBN 9781913679477

Edited by Krystyna Mayer
Designed by Nigel Partridge

Printed and bound in Malaysia by Times Offset (M) Sdn. Bhd.

·Contents·

Introduction 4

Why Enjoy Butterflies? 4

About Butterflies 6

The Origins of Butterflies 7

Butterfly Physical Characteristics 8

Butterfly Family Trees 9

Butterflies in Hong Kong 10

A Closer Look – Special Patterns 11

Organization of Species Descriptions 12

Glossary 12

Species Descriptions 15

Checklist of the Butterflies of Hong Kong 164

Acknowledgements 172

Further Reading 173

Index 174

INTRODUCTION

If you ever enjoyed a walk outside or felt curious about the millions of flying, hopping or growing creatures that we share this planet with, then this book is for you. As a window on Hong Kong and its natural treasures, the book provides detailed guidance on finding and identifying the 235 most commonly seen butterflies in Hong Kong, representing >99.9 per cent of the 124,000 plus Hong Kong butterfly sightings posted to iNaturalist (p. 173). Each of these 235 species had at least seven sightings posted on iNaturalist as of October 2023. Also listed are 28 very rare or vagrant species that are not found in Hong Kong every year but may be worth keeping an eye out for. With practice, this book will enable you to identify almost all the adult butterflies you see in Hong Kong, whether female or male, of any species. The text includes details on when and where to find butterflies, and the food-plant notes provide a broader naturalist perspective, to glimpse the interconnected ecology of these insects and where they fit in the broader web of life. The author's goal is to enable those who read this book, of whatever age or background, to have more fun than they did before (yes, butterflies can do that) and a deeper appreciation of life and our place in this world.

WHY ENJOY BUTTERFLIES?

Just when the caterpillar thought the world was over, it became a butterfly.
Attributed to Chuang Tzu

Butterflies are miracles of life. They can capture your imagination and lift you from the daily grind, as they have millions of people throughout the ages. How is it that this bundle of inanimate star dust, starting as a crawling worm, eating ordinary leaves, can defy gravity and transform into dancing colour?

Without any schooling or parental instruction, consider how and why a particular caterpillar only eats from one tree type, and not from another. And on a certain day and at a

Compare the Common Archduke larva on the left, complete with spines and orange balls, to the adult butterfly on the right, a transformation that occurs over just a couple of weeks.

Why Enjoy Butterflies?

certain time hang itself up like a dress, digest itself into soup, then, over just a week or two, reorganize its cells into an animate 'kite'. One that can migrate in one direction for hundreds of kilometres, recognize and attract the opposite sex of its own kind, even though it looks different from it, and sip, soar and bask for the blink of an eye before death returns it to the soil just a few weeks later. At which point its offspring may be munching on that same tree to do it all again. May we never forget that this is nearly unbelievable.

Why do so many people enjoy butterflies?

A window into the past Beyond the artistic beauty of these animals, learning about butterflies provides a fresh, new perspective. Why are these 235 butterfly species found in Hong Kong today? Why not 714 others? Why are there so many more in Hong Kong than the 55 or so found in the United Kingdom, despite a much smaller area? The short answer: a combination of Earth's history, biological evolution (what evolved where, and when) and human choices.

A lens to better understand the world as it is As humans we naturally walk around with a human-centred perspective, a very small slice of reality. Just as we can better understand our mother tongue by learning a second language, delving into butterflies can broaden our perspective and increase our enjoyment of the world. Areas that were invisible can surprise us with their richness. One practical example involves ultraviolet light, which is all around us but is not apparent to our primate eyes. Butterflies can see this light, invisible to us, and some flowers even evolved markings that shine in ultraviolet light, beckoning butterflies to come hither. This applies at a deeper level as well, beyond our physical sight. Learning the butterflies of Hong Kong can be an exercise in learning to see what is all around us, but easily missed. Just like the moments of our everyday lives. The fragility and change in butterfly populations, which are dependent on specific plants and sufficient clean land, air and water, are a good reminder of our human dependence on these same, sustainable resources. By caring for butterflies, we care for ourselves.

Exercise and community Learning about butterflies could improve your health, and butterfly lovers tend to be friendly, or interesting or both. There are worse ways to spend your time than enjoying the outdoors, moving your body. While outside it can be fun and helpful to have a focus, whether on architecture, birds or butterflies. Many in Hong Kong enjoy how 'going to the butterflies' takes you to surprising, unseen corners. These undiscovered gems enable you to meet the city you think you already know again, afresh. Hiking outdoors is enjoyment of a sustainable resource, and is a good family activity, away from electronic screens, at a slower pace.

Professional performance and happiness Noticing butterflies is a habit that you can develop like any other. Many have discovered that if they can pause, even for 30 minutes a week, to notice the butterflies around them, when they return to work and family, they bring greater clarity, creativity and calm. This can combat burnout and improve their professional focus. More and more doctors and coaches 'prescribe' unplugged time outdoors for renewal and sustained wellbeing.

It is just fun Butterflies offer fun and challenge on a sliding scale for almost everyone. You can easily pick up a couple of things about a few species in just 15 minutes, yet there are always new frontiers to challenge the experts as well.

About Butterflies

About Butterflies

Butterflies are multicellular animals (insects), not as different as you might think from us humans. Each begins life as a tiny fertilized egg and focuses its time on getting enough food, water and shelter. Butterflies also avoid danger and find a partner to successfully create the next generation. They use sight, smell, touch and even hearing to move towards helpful things and away from harmful threats. They use nerves and muscles, navigate a home area that is familiar and need to rest.

Of course, there are differences between humans and butterflies. Our bodies are larger and sprout only four limbs, rather than 10 (four wings plus six legs). Unlike animals with backbones, butterflies have a hard, external skeleton made of the protein chitin. While human bodies are hard on the inside (bony skeleton) and softer on the outside, jointed arthropod animals, like butterflies and other insects, crustaceans and spiders, are hard on the outside and soft on the inside. However, they share many of our same parts, including a digestive tract, a breathing system and reproductive organs.

When it comes to reproduction, like us butterflies use internal fertilization (with a penis-like appendage inserted in the female to release sperm and fertilize an egg). However, partly because of the hard external skeleton (which cannot easily expand with growing babies), the butterfly lays her fertilized egg (usually just one) to develop *outside* her body. Through intricate chemistry and co-evolution with plants, she can 'taste' different plants with her feet and proboscis 'tongue' to identify a good food source for her offspring. After just a few days, the new caterpillar, or larva, eats a hole in the egg wall and 'hatches' into the world. The main focus of its life is growth, which requires food. Some species can eat many types of plant, and others eat just 1–2. Roughly two-thirds of butterfly caterpillars only feed on one plant family. Some caterpillars specifically eat poisonous plants so that they will be bitter and distasteful to birds and other predators. They have invented a novel way to 'store' the poisons in their body but avoid getting poisoned themselves. This is a useful development, especially interesting because the plant developed the poison to deter caterpillars and other animals from eating it. Another useful development is that the caterpillar food (plant leaves) is different from the adult food (mainly flower nectar or fruits), so that parent and offspring do not compete with each other for the same food supply.

The butterfly life cycle involves four stages: the egg, larva (caterpillar), pupa (chrysalis) and adult (imago). Butterflies share this strategy with other 'advanced', or holometabolous, insects like beetles and bees. After a few days as an egg, a caterpillar develops through around five stages, or instars, typically over a few days for each instar. At the end of each stage, it sheds its skin to allow growth to the next, larger size. Thus after 15–30 days of being a caterpillar, it spins a small silken pad and sheds its final skin to reveal a chrysalis. Six to 16 days later the adult butterfly emerges from this cocoon. It stretches out its wings and is ready to fly. While the lifespan can vary, generally adult butterflies live for 15–30 days – such a brief window of time. Many Hong Kong butterflies have more than one generation in a calendar year, and if you develop awareness you can sense the cycles – first noticing the caterpillars, then the adults. Later the adults disappear for a while, before another wave appears a month or two later.

Butterflies employ a few other tricks to successfully reproduce. For example, males often establish small territories in prominent locations, like a hilltop. They perch assertively at the edge of this territory, chasing away rivals and attempting to woo passing females. This approach brings advantages for the female as well. Rather than having to fly all over town, in this way she has an easier time finding and comparing potential mates. Sometimes this 'hilltopping' behaviour can turn frenetic, almost like a singles bar, with lots of back-and-forth communication, mingling and even dancing. If the female likes how the male makes her feel, she accepts his advances and they mate. And on the cycle goes.

To prepare for these sessions and maintain their fitness, males take time out to mudpuddle, often with other males. Mudpuddling involves finding a patch of wet ground and drinking up salty mineral water. The salts are naturally found in the soil but remain inaccessible until dissolved in rainwater. This is critical nutrition, because nectar, the main butterfly food, brings the calories but lacks the minerals needed for sperm formation.

Some male butterflies have, however, found a way to gain more than just energy from nectar. That from certain plants, especially those in the sunflower (Asteraceae) family, contains special chemicals called pyrrolizidine alkaloids. These molecules are useful in the manufacture of the pheromones that males release into the air, like cologne, to attract females. These alkaloids can also be used as bitter toxins that provide protection from predators. Taken together, between mudpuddling and seeking out special nectar, male butterflies have successfully addressed three of life's basic challenges: get enough to eat, do not get eaten yourself (certain plant nectar) and grow a family (between the pheromones, then mudpuddling to make healthy sperm). Add some hilltopping to bring the sexes together, and we can now trace the outline of an adult butterfly's life.

A butterfly's behaviour provides valuable clues as to its identity. Specific areas to note are: activity period (daytime vs. dusk), flight style (slow vs. fast, high above vs. low to the ground), posture at rest (with wings held closed, or opened flat, or with a skipper-type jet position). Several butterflies are also distinctive in feeding on fruit or other non-flower food sources.

THE ORIGINS OF BUTTERFLIES

Butterflies did not exist for most of Earth's history. Butterflies are technically a group of moths – mainly colourful, day-flying moths in the scientific insect order Lepidoptera. From what we can tell, the first Lepidoptera moths evolved from older insects around 200 million years ago, just as the Jurassic Period began. These moths adapted to a changing world, leading to the first butterflies (as a subset of moths) about 108 million years ago. This means they did not overlap with beasts of the deep past, like *Dunkleosteus* or *Stegosaurus*. However, they are much older than *Tyrannasaurus rex* and there is a good chance that they flew past munching *Triceratops*.

In sum, butterflies have only existed for the last 2–3 per cent of Earth's history. If you map this on to a 24-hour day, then butterflies first appeared at around 11.26 p.m., just 34 minutes before midnight. This period coincided with the rapid growth of broadleaved trees and especially flowers (with that energy-packed nectar) during the Cretaceous Period. The best evidence suggests that butterflies originated in western North America and

■ Butterfly Physical Characteristics ■

first came to Asia via Alaska about 75 million years ago, before radiating into many new species in tropical Asia. Butterflies have achieved spectacular success, and now live almost everywhere. Current estimates total 19,000 butterfly species in the world today, more than all bird and mammal species combined.

Butterfly Physical Characteristics

Each butterfly comprises the usual insect body parts, including head, thorax (with three segments) and abdomen (with 10 segments). The thorax provides the muscle attachments for three pairs of legs and two pairs of wings. When looking at a butterfly, the two forewings and two hindwings have several edges, called margins: first the base (where the wing attaches to the body), the costal margin (the front edge) leading to the apex (wingtip), and the outer wing edge, called the termen. Digging deeper, wings can be divided into several regions. One useful sequence starts at the base and progresses outwards as follows: base, then postbasal, subdiscal, discal, postdiscal, submarginal and marginal area at the outer edge. The lower rear corner of the hindwing is called the tornus and often sports false eyes (called eye-spots) and false antennae (called wing-tails), especially in gossamer-winged butterflies (family Lycaenidae).

Butterflies with these false head parts often move the hindwings up and down to simulate a nodding head. Scientists think that this strategy can distract predators from biting at the butterfly's real head, allowing escape with the key bits intact.

The butterfly sizes in the text correlate to the wingspans given, with slight modification

Butterfly anatomy

Butterfly Family Trees

by family. As a general guideline, small: WS 20–35mm, medium: 35–50mm (to 70mm for Nymphalidae) and large: WS 50 (for Hesperiidae) to 100mm.

Butterfly Family Trees

The scientific consensus groups butterflies into seven groups of related species, or families, of which six (235 species) are found in Hong Kong. The earliest family to evolve is most similar to other moths, before the swallowtails and other families appeared. Families are divided into subfamilies (of even closer relatives), subfamilies into tribes (and subtribes), genera, then species and subspecies. It can be useful to note 'family resemblances' between relatives.

As an example, the 21 Hong Kong swallowtail species all belong to the same family, and even the same subfamily. The next subdivison is the tribe. For example, there are three tribes of Hong Kong swallowtail, pictured and outlined in this book.

Below is a brief overview of each family, including an informal common name (which can vary) and the official scientific family name (which is fixed and generally does not change). The common and scientific names used in this book are based on the iNaturalist website and the Hong Kong Government website.

Hedylidae (American Moth-butterflies) Small and brown, without clubbed antennae. The oldest group, today found in North and South America, with greatest diversity in southern Peru. Not found in Hong Kong.

Papilionidae (Swallowtails) Tail-like wing projections, sailing or fluttering flight, wings usually remain fluttering while feeding. Three pairs of legs. Found worldwide, and Hong Kong may be the best major city in the world to see a wide variety of this spectacular family. For comparison, Singapore has about 14 species, Miami four, Paris two, London one, Rio de Janeiro 13, New York City five, Manila six, Sydney four, Beijing eight, Mumbai 10, Cape Town one. Species in HK: 21.

Hedylidae

Papilionidae

Hesperiidae (Skippers) Small, with darting flight. Often perch like little jets, with forewings held aloft and hindwings at the horizontal. Antennae placed widely apart on head, and hooked at ends. Found

Hesperiidae

Pieridae

■ Butterflies in Hong Kong ■

Nymphalidae

Riodinidae

Lycaenidae

worldwide. Species in HK: 59.

Pieridae (Whites & Yellows) White or yellow in colour, often with black markings. Whites usually rest with wings open, and yellows with wings closed. Rapid, fluttering flight. Three pairs of legs. Found worldwide. Species in HK: 17.

Nymphalidae (Brush-footed Butterflies) Large and diverse family, though surprisingly both sexes only have four developed legs (rather than the usual six). Found worldwide. Species in HK: 78.

Riodinidae (Metalmark Butterflies) Closely related to gossamer-winged butterflies, in Hong Kong these butterflies often flutter and prance, turning leaves into a dance floor. Females have three pairs of developed legs, males only two. Found worldwide. Species in HK: three.

Lycaenidae (Gossamer-winged Butterflies) Small butterflies with rapid, fluttering flight. Often blue above and spotted below, with an orange spot at the lower corner of the hindwing and a short wing-tail. Found worldwide. Species in HK: 57.

BUTTERFLIES IN HONG KONG

When you walk outside in Hong Kong, a subtropical city of 7.4 million people covering 2,755 km^2, there are roughly 235 butterfly species to enjoy. This fabulous array is justly famous – as mentioned above, Hong Kong hosts the highest number of swallowtail species of any major city in the world. In fact, the creator of James Bond, Ian Fleming, marvelled at the butterflies of Hong Kong in his mid-century book *Thrilling Cities* after a visit to the Fragrant Harbour. Although Hong Kong covers <0.03 per cent of the land area of China, this jewel of a city hosts more than 11 per cent of the 2,100 Chinese butterflies.

Positioned just within the tropics at 22.3 degrees north of the Equator and 114.2 degrees east of the Prime Meridian, it was not preordained that these 235 species would make up the Hong Kong butterfly fauna today. The combination of species stems from many apparently random causes over tens of millions of years, as well as human actions over the last few thousand years. In other words, this assemblage of species is *contingent*, based on specific but unplanned events over a long period of time.

Despite this contingency, patterns may be found among Hong Kong butterflies. While

A Closer Look – Special Patterns

these 235 species represent a melting pot of derivates from many sources (some came from the west, others from the north and so on), careful examination reveals a consistent pattern. Think of it like this: when scientists survey Earth's land and mark boundaries around where related plants and animals are found, they notice a consistent set of eight areas. That is, the Earth can be organized into eight centres of related biodiversity, called biogeographic realms, which roughly correlate with continents.

There are therefore shared similarities in the plants and animals across South America, but major differences versus Sub-Saharan Africa. Thus South America (termed the Neotropical realm) and Sub-Saharan Africa (sometimes called the Afrotropical realm) represent two of the eight biogeographic realms. Hong Kong is positioned in what is termed the Indomalayan realm. This region of similar plants and animals extends from the Indian subcontinent in the west to southern China in the north-east, to Borneo, the Philippines and Bali in the south-east. This happens to map fairly closely to the original range of the Asian Elephant, which formerly roamed the subtropical forests of Hong Kong. If you check the species descriptions, by far the most common range listed for Hong Kong butterflies stretches from India to southern China, through mainland Southeast Asia, to Borneo and the Philippines. There are some intriguing exceptions, with a few species extending west to Africa or east into the Pacific, ranging as far as Tahiti or Hawaii. The widest range in this book belongs to the Painted Lady, which is nearly global in distribution except for Australia, South America and Antarctica. There are also a few species with much smaller ranges, including those limited to southern China, and one skipper subspecies only known in Hong Kong itself.

In sum, most species of Hong Kong butterfly may be classified as Indomalayan species. The main exceptions are those from the neighbouring biogeographic region to the north, the Palearctic realm – for instance, the Chinese Yellow Swallowtail, which ranges from Hong Kong north to central and northern China, south-east Siberia, Korea and Japan. The Chestnut Tiger Butterfly is another example, with northern populations in Japan migrating south to Hong Kong in winter.

Among the many good areas to find butterflies in Hong Kong, here are a few that merit multiple visits, preferably in different seasons:
- Wu Kau Tang and Lai Chi Wo
- Fung Yuen Butterfly Reserve
- Shing Mun Country Park
- Tai Po Kau Nature Reserve
- Pak Tam Chung Family Walk
- Ngong Ping
- Kap Lung Ancient Trail
- The Peak
- Lung Kwu Tan

A Closer Look – Special Patterns

Beyond geographic range, an analysis of these 235 species reveals several intriguing

Organization of Species Descriptions

patterns. Here is one: though the vast majority of these butterflies are diurnal in habit, around 12 species are crepuscular, especially active at dusk. These 12, mainly skippers, include: Indian Awlking, Orange Red Skirt, Pale Green Awlet, Branded Orange Awlet, Common Awl, Slate Awl, Common Redeye, Rounded Palm-Redeye, Plain Palm Dart, Common Palmfly, Common Evening Brown, and Dark Evening Brown. This evening lifestyle quirk is worth noting if you would like to find these special butterflies.

Another pattern: while 209 species mainly feed on nectar as adults, in 26 species the adults focus on other foods, such as fruit: Tawny Rajah, Yellow Rajah, Common Nawab, Shan t, Great Nawab, Common Palmfly, Large Faun, Common Duffer, Common Evening Brown, Dark Evening Brown, Dark-branded Bushbrown, South China Bushbrown, Banded Treebrown, Bamboo Treebrown, Common Treebrown, Angled Red Forester, Black-spotted Labyrinth, Gaudy Baron, Common Baron, White-edged Blue Baron, Green Skirt Baron, Common Archduke, Constable, Common Mapwing, Blue Admiral, and Forest Pierrot. Note that all but one of these species are Brush-footed Butterflies.

In only two species, both Harvesters, caterpillars do not feed on plants at all but eat aphids.

At least 11 species of Gossamer-winged Butterflies have ants that attend the caterpillars, generally protecting them from predators and in exchange sipping a honeydew-like liquid from the caterpillars.

At least three of Hong Kong's butterflies were introduced by humans, generally with landscaping plants: Small Cabbage White, Common Palmfly and Plains Cupid. While the majority of Hong Kong species are resident most of the year, 16 species are known to migrate: 1 skipper, 5 pierids, 9 Brush-footed Butterflies, plus 1 lycaenid. 226 species lay a single egg, but in at least 9 species the female lays a cluster of eggs all together: Chinese Windmill, Three-spotted Grass Yellow, Red-based Jezebel, Painted Jezebel, Large Faun, Common Duffer, Black-spotted Labyrinth, Common Jester and Spotted Royal.

21 species are known to harbour toxins that make them distasteful to birds and other predators. And lastly, at least 12 species mimic these toxic species to reduce predation, copying the colour patterns of toxic butterflies to fool birds into leaving them alone: 4 swallowtails plus 8 Brush-footed Butterflies.

At least six plant species in Hong Kong could not survive without butterflies and moths visiting their flowers: Splash-of-White *Mussaenda pubescens* and Hong Kong Pavetta *Pavetta hongkongensis* in the Coffee (Rubiaceae) family, Glabrous Pittosporum *Pittosporum glabratum* in the Pittosporum (Pittosporaceae) family, Acronychia *Acronychia pedunculata* in the Citrus (Rutaceae) family, Long-flowered Ehretia *Ehretia longiflora* in the Borage (Boraginaceae) family and Reevesia *Reevesia thyrsoidea* in the Mallow (Malvaceae) family.

The climate is slowly changing and this impact can be seen in local butterfly populations. A warming climate is driving the ranges of tropical species northward at a fairly rapid rate, roughly 10–20km per year. As local weather becomes more like Southeast Asia, recent years have brought several new butterflies to Hong Kong, including Sullied Brown Sailer (since around 2017), Common Line Blue (2018), Small Yellow Sailer (2019), Princess Flash (2019), Lesser Gull (2021), Fluffy Tit (2021), Silver Royal (2021) and Great Nawab (2021).

Glossary

Organization of Species Descriptions

A standard structure has been used for the species descriptions. The species are arranged in rough chronological order, with the groups that evolved longest ago at the beginning, and the more recent groups at the end. A basic description is given for each species. Where applicable, comparisons between sexes and with other Hong Kong species have been included, as have variations in forms, such as wet-season form and dry-season form. Under distribution, incidence in Hong Kong is given first, followed by a brief note on distribution elsewhere. Habitat and behavioural habits are covered, as are adult and larval food plants, and behaviour characteristics applicable to particular species.

Abbreviations used are as follows: HK (Hong Kong); HKI (Hong Kong Island); NT (New Territories); SE Asia (Southeast Asia); WS (wingspan).

Glossary

anterior Towards the front, or head. Contrast with **posterior**.
base Part of wing where it attaches to body. Contrast with **wing apex**.
basking When a butterfly rests in sunshine, often with wings spread open. May be used to warm up the animal, to help regulate its body temperature.
canopy Higher part of a forest, at level of treetops.
caterpillar Larval stage of a butterfly, between egg and pupal (chrysalis) stages. Worm-like, with a focus on feeding and growth. Also known as larva.
costa Leading edge, or margin, of a wing.
crepuscular Mainly active at dusk and dawn. Contrast with **diurnal**.
diurnal Mainly active in by day. Contrast with **crepuscular**.
ecology Study of relationships and interactions between different types of organism in the environment.
evolution Change of a group of organisms, typically slowly and over a long period of time, from one state to another. Often occuring in response to changes in the environment, evolution can result in the formation of new species. The most useful and powerful biological framework for explaining how, why and where particular lifeforms are found, and making sense of the tree of life, both today and in the past.
eye-spots Spots of colour on wing, typically dark with a lighter border. Thought to be protective by startling or distracting predators from true eyes.
family Group of relatively closely related genera (or species). May be divided into subfamilies, then tribes, subtribes and genera, then species.
food plant Also known as larval host plant, main food source for caterpillar of a particular butterfly species. Typically, the leaves of a certain family (group) of plants, for instance the citrus (Rutaceae) family. A few adult butterflies are also particular about the types of flower they sip nectar from. For example, some male milkweed butterflies (Nymphalidae subfamily Danainae) feed on nectar from Rattlepod *Crotolaria* and Goatweed *Ageratum* plants in the sunflower (Asteraceae) family. Males then convert toxins found in this unusual nectar (pyrrolizidine alkaloids) into sex pheromones to attract females.
forewing Front wing on each side of a butterfly. Contrast with **hindwing**.

Glossary

genus (pl **genera**) Group of closely related species, all species in the genus having evolved from a shared, common ancestor in the not too distant past.
habitat Type of vegetation, for example freshwater wetland, hill forest, coastal scrub or grassland.
hilltopping Tendency of male butterflies of many species to congregate at prominent points in a landscape, especially hilltops. Females often visit these areas as well, since they provide a convenient location to find a mate.
hindwing Rear wing on each side of a butterfly. Contrast with **forewing**.
margin Edge of a wing.
marginal Markings near wing edge. Contrast with **submarginal**.
mimic Non-toxic butterfly species that has evolved to look similar to a bitter, toxic butterfly to reduce predation. In addition to looking like the toxic model, mimics can also modify their behaviour to further increase the resemblance. Contrast with **model**.
model Butterfly species that feeds on toxic plants to become poisonous and distasteful to predators, which reduces predation. The colour patterns (and even behaviour) may be copied by **mimics**.
mudpuddling When butterflies, especially males, land on damp ground and sip salt-laden moisture for nutrition.
nectar Sweet, sugary liquid found in most flowers. Main food source for adult butterflies.
posterior Away from head, towards abdomen. Contrast with **anterior**.
secondary woodland Open or semi-open habitat of medium-height shrubs and trees, where the original (primary) forest was previously cut down. Over time, naturally grows taller and more complex.
species A 'type' of organism. Interbreeds freely within population of its own kind, but generally not with other types of butterfly. Closely related species are grouped into the same genus. The scientific name of a species has two words – the genus, then the species. For example, the Spangle Swallowtail is known as *Papilio protenor*, denoting species '*protenor*' and genus '*Papilio*'.
submarginal Refers to wing markings placed at slight distance from wing margin. Contrast with **marginal**.
territory Area of ground or vegetation patrolled by a male butterfly to exclude other males. Territorial male typically attempts to mate with passing females.
underside Lower or ventral surface of wings. When a butterfly rests with wings closed (held up), underside surface is visible from sides.
upperside Top or dorsal surface of wings. When a butterfly rests with wings open (held down), upperside surface is visible from above.
termen Lateral edge, or margin, of a wing.
tornus Outer, lower corner of hindwing. Can often have wing-tails or orange eye-spots.
vagrant Rare visitor to an area. Vagrants are typically 'lost' or blown off course by severe weather. Occasionally they may persist in a new location and establish a viable population.
wing apex Front, outer corner of forewing.
wing-tail Projection from trailing edge of hindwing, especially in swallowtails and gossamer-winged butterflies.

■ PAPILIONIDAE ■

Tailed Jay ■ *Graphium agamemnon* 統帥青鳳蝶 WS 70–80mm

DESCRIPTION Brown above and brown below, with green spots and short tail. Sexes similar. **DISTRIBUTION** Common in HKI, NT and Lantau. Otherwise found from India to southern China, through SE Asia, to eastern Indonesia and Australia. **HABITAT AND HABITS** Often seen in parks, gardens and other open areas at low elevation; attracted to flowering shrubs. Flight swift and skipping, rarely settling. Adults sip nectar, fluttering wings constantly. Caterpillars feed on *Desmos*, *Uvaria* and *Artabotrys* in custard apple (Annonaceae) family and *Magnolia* trees in magnolia (Magnoliaceae) family. Seen Mar–Nov.

Common Jay ■ *Graphium doson* 木蘭青鳳蝶 WS 55–60mm

DESCRIPTION Black above and brown below, with large, pale spots that range from yellow to pale green or turquoise above and below. Smaller than Tailed Jay (above), with no tail on hindwing. Differs from Common Bluebottle (p. 16) at rest by having multiple rows of light spots below. Sexes similar. **DISTRIBUTION** Fairly common in HKI, NT and Lantau. Otherwise found from India to southern China, through mainland SE Asia, to Borneo and the Philippines. **HABITAT AND HABITS** Occurs in wooded areas, usually at low elevation, though males may hilltop. Attracted to flowering shrubs. Flight swift and skipping, rarely settling. Adults sip nectar, fluttering wings constantly. Caterpillars feed on Chinese Desmos *Desmos chinensis*, *Uvaria* in custard apple (Annonaceae) family and White Jade Orchid Tree *Magnolia* (*Michelia*) x *alba* in magnolia (Magnoliaceae) family. Seen Mar–Nov, especially July and Aug.

▪ Papilionidae ▪

Five-bar Swordtail ▪ *Graphium (Pathysa) antiphates* 綠鳳蝶 WS 70–80mm

DESCRIPTION Pale yellow with black stripes. Long, slender wing-tail distinctive, but when missing can appear like a fast pierid butterfly. Sexes similar. **DISTRIBUTION** Fairly common in HKI; uncommon in NT and Lantau. Otherwise found from India to southern China, through mainland SE Asia to Borneo. **HABITAT AND HABITS** Occurs in wooded areas, primarily at low elevations. Flight rapid and direct. Adults sip nectar, and males may visit wet mud. Caterpillars feed on Chinese Desmos *Desmos chinensis* and *Uvaria* in custard apple (Annonaceae) family, and White Jade Orchid Tree *Magnolia* (*Michelia*) x *alba* in magnolia (Magnoliaceae) family. Seen Mar–Nov, especially Apr–May.

Common Bluebottle ▪ *Graphium sarpedon* 青鳳蝶 WS 75–85mm

DESCRIPTION Wings long and pointed; black above and brown below, with broad turquoise band and no tail on hindwing. Sexes similar. **DISTRIBUTION** Common in HKI, NT and Lantau. Otherwise found from India to central and southern China, through mainland SE Asia. **HABITAT AND HABITS** Occurs in wooded areas at all elevations. Flight rapid and direct, often high at canopy level. Adults sip nectar, and males may visit wet mud and hilltops. Caterpillars feed on *Cinnamomum*, *Litsea* and *Persea* plants in laurel (Lauraceae) family. Seen Feb–Nov, especially May and Oct.

▪ Papilionidae ▪

Glassy Bluebottle ▪ *Graphium cloanthus* 寬帶青鳳蝶 WS 75–85mm

DESCRIPTION Wings long and pointed, black above and brown below, with broad turquoise band and tail on hindwing. Compared to similar Common Bluebottle (p. 16), also shows additional turquoise spots on forewing. Sexes similar. **DISTRIBUTION** Not seen in HKI or Lantau; fairly common in NT. Otherwise found from India to central and southern China, through mainland SE Asia. **HABITAT AND HABITS** Occurs in wooded areas, usually at higher elevations. Flight rapid and direct, often high at canopy level. Adults sip nectar, and males may visit wet mud and hilltops. Caterpillars feed on *Persea* plants in laurel (Lauraceae) family. Seen Mar–Sep.

White Dragontail Butterfly ▪ *Lamproptera curius* 燕鳳蝶 WS 35–40mm

DESCRIPTION Distinctive – unlike any other HK butterfly and one of the smallest swallowtails in the world. Forewing transparent in centre, with black margin. Very long wing-tail. Male slightly darker than female but otherwise sexes similar. **DISTRIBUTION** Rare in HKI and Lantau; uncommon in NT. Otherwise found from India to southern China, through mainland Southeast Asia. **HABITAT AND HABITS** Occurs in wooded areas, especially along streams, where may be found mudpuddling. Flight unusually rocking and buzzing, and can fly backwards. Adults sip nectar, especially from *Vitex negundo*. Caterpillars feed on *Illigera celebica* in Hernandia (Hernandiaceae) family. Seen Feb–Nov, especially June–July.

■ PAPILIONIDAE ■

Common Rose Swallowtail ■ *Pachliopta aristolochiae* 紅珠鳳蝶
WS 90–100mm

DESCRIPTION Wings black with grey highlights, with white patches on hindwing and red marginal spots below. Body a distinctive pinkish-red. Sexes similar. Toxic due to chemicals absorbed from host plant as a caterpillar, including aristolochic acid. This successful strategy has led to mimicking by other swallowtails, including the female Great Mormon Swallowtail (p. 22), form *achates*, and female Common Mormon Swallowtail (p. 21), form *polytes*. Red Helen Swallowtail (p. 25) also similar. These best distinguished by their black bodies, though hindwing-underside differs subtly, and Red Helen also lacks grey forewing highlights. DISTRIBUTION Fairly common in HKI and NT; uncommon in Lantau. Otherwise found from India to central and southern China, through mainland SE Asia. HABITAT AND HABITS Occurs in wooded areas. Flight slow and often high. Adults sip nectar. Caterpillars feed on Indian Birthwort *Aristolochia acuminata* (*tagala*) and *A. fordiana* in birthwort (Aristolochiaceae) family. Seen Apr–Oct.

Chinese Windmill ■ *Byasa confusa* 中華麝鳳蝶 WS 80–90mm

DESCRIPTION Body distinctive pinkish-red. Hindwing narrow and black, with long, narrow wing-tail and red margin spots. No white hindwing-patches. Forewing black (male) or black with grey highlights (female). DISTRIBUTION Rare in HKI, almost exclusively in Mount Nicholson area; not seen in NT and Lantau. Otherwise only found in central and southeastern China. HABITAT AND HABITS Occurs in wooded areas. Flight slow. Adults sip nectar, and males seen chasing away rivals. Female lays eggs in clusters, unique among HK swallowtails. Caterpillars feed on *Aristolochia* plants in birthwort (Aristolochiaceae) family. Adults seen Apr–Aug, especially May.

■ PAPILIONIDAE ■

Golden Birdwing ■ *Troides aeacus* 金裳鳳蝶 WS 100–150mm

DESCRIPTION Largest butterfly in China. Forewing black and hindwing yellow, with no wing-tail. Often larger than Common Birdwing (below), and Golden male lacks black hindwing-spots, with greyish-yellow along margin. Golden female has additional yellow spot near hindwing-base, and hindwing-spots more triangular (less round) than in Common. Black spots on yellow abdomen typically larger in Golden. Male notably smaller than female. **DISTRIBUTION** Uncommon in HKI, NT and Lantau. Otherwise found from India to central and southern China, through mainland SE Asia. **HABITAT AND HABITS** Occurs in wooded areas. Flight fairly slow. Often seen gliding high in canopy. Adults sip nectar. Caterpillars feed on Indian Birthwort *Aristolochia acuminata* (*tagala*) in birthwort (Aristolochiaceae) family. Seen Apr–Nov.

Male

Female

Common Birdwing ■ *Troides helena* 裳鳳蝶 WS 105–130mm

Mating pair, with female at top

Female

DESCRIPTION Forewing black and hindwing yellow, with no tail. Often smaller than Golden Birdwing (above), and Common male has at least one black hindwing-spot, without greyish-yellow along margin. Golden female has additional yellow spot near hindwing-base, and hindwing-spots rounder in Common. Black spots on yellow abdomen typically smaller in Common. Male notably smaller than female. **DISTRIBUTION** Rare in HKI, fairly common in NT; not seen in Lantau. Otherwise found from India to southern China, through mainland SE Asia, to eastern Indonesia. **HABITAT AND HABITS** Occurs in wooded areas. Flight fairly slow; often seen gliding high in canopy. Adults sip nectar, often from *Lantana* flowers, and male may actively patrol territory along forest paths. Caterpillars feed on Indian Birthwort *Aristolochia acuminata* (*tagala*) and *A. fordiana* in birthwort (Aristolochiaceae) family. Seen Mar–Dec, especially June–Oct.

▪ PAPILIONIDAE ▪

Common Mime Swallowtail ▪ *Papilio clytia* 斑鳳蝶 WS 90–105mm

DESCRIPTION Occurs in two forms. Most common *dissimilis* form, which mimics the toxic Blue Tiger (p. 74), black and white with orange marginal hindwing-spots below. Less common *clytia* form, mainly black with similar orange hindwing spotting, mimics toxic Blue-spotted Crow (p. 78), even copying its behaviour (for example hanging to roost from dead branches with wings closed). No wing-tail, and sexes similar. **DISTRIBUTION** Fairly common in HKI, NT and Lantau. Otherwise found from India to central and southern China, through mainland SE Asia, to Borneo and the Philippines. **HABITAT AND HABITS** Occurs in shrubby areas and gardens at a range of elevations. Flight slow and similar to danaid milkweed butterflies. Adults sip nectar, and males often aggressively defend hilltop territories. Caterpillars feed on Bolly Beech *Litsea glutinosa* and Camphor Tree *Cinnamomum camphora* in laurel (Lauraceae) family. Seen year round, especially May–Oct.

dissimilis

clytia

Tawny Mime Swallowtail ▪ *Papilio agestor* 褐斑鳳蝶 WS 90–100mm

DESCRIPTION Black and white with tawny orange on hindwing, including underside. Mimics toxic Chestnut Tiger (p. 76), though present species has more black wing-veins and grey speckling in white cells. No wing-tail, and sexes similar. **DISTRIBUTION** Uncommon. Not seen in HKI and Lantau; uncommon in NT (mainly in Tai Po Kau area). Otherwise found from India to southern China, through mainland SE Asia. **HABITAT AND HABITS** Occurs in wooded uplands. Flight slow, often above canopy, and mimicking *Parantica* milkweed butterflies. Adults sip nectar, and males often aggressively defends hilltop territories. Caterpillars feed on Cinnamon *Cinnamomum*, *Machilus* and *Persea* plants in laurel (Lauraceae) family. Only one brood per year, and almost exclusively seen in Mar.

PAPILIONIDAE

Common Mormon Swallowtail ■ *Papilio polytes* 玉帶鳳蝶
WS 80–90mm

DESCRIPTION Most common swallowtail in urban areas and gardens. Wings black with white band, and wing-tail. Female of common form *mandale* similar to male, with marginal red spots below on hindwing. Female of uncommon form *polytes* mimics toxic Common Rose Swallowtail (p. 18), but lacks pink body, and white hindwing-band replaced by white patch and more red marginal spotting. **DISTRIBUTION** Common in HKI, NT and Lantau. Otherwise found from India to southern China, through mainland SE Asia, to Borneo, the Philippines and eastern Indonesia, to Mariana Islands. **HABITAT AND HABITS** Occurs widely in forest edges, gardens and citrus orchards in lowlands. Flight moderately strong, though *polytes* females have slower flight that mimics Common Rose. Adults sip nectar. Caterpillars feed on Pomelo *Citrus maxima*, Sweet Orange *C.* x *sinensis*, Lemon *C.* x *limon*, Wampi *Clausena lansium* and Orange Jessamine *Murraya paniculata* in citrus (Rutaceae) family. Seen all year, with May peak.

Female form mandale

Female form polytes

PAPILIONIDAE

Great Mormon Swallowtail ■ *Papilio memnon* 美鳳蝶 WS 110–130mm

Male

Male

Female form agenor

Female form achates

DESCRIPTION Large common swallowtail. Male black with blue metallic sheen and no tail. Compared to similar Spangle Swallowtail (opposite), male has shorter hindwing and wing-base bright red below. Female variable – common form *agenor* has greyish forewing, red wing-bases above and below, and white hindwing-patch with no tail. Female of uncommon form *achates* mimics toxic Common Rose Swallowtail (p. 18) above (but lacks pink body), and is similar to form *agenor* but with less white and more red on hindwing, plus wing-tail. **DISTRIBUTION** Common in HKI, NT and Lantau. Otherwise found from India to southern China, through mainland SE Asia, to Borneo, the Philippines and Japan. **HABITAT AND HABITS** Occurs in lowland woodland, parks and citrus orchards. Flight erratic and sailing. Adults sip nectar. Caterpillars feed on Pomelo *Citrus maxima*, Mandarin *C. reticulata*, Sweet Orange *C.* x *sinensis*, Kumquat *C.* (*Fortunella*) *japonica* and *hindsii*, and Wampi *Clausena lansium* in citrus (Rutaceae) family. Seen Mar–Dec.

■ PAPILIONIDAE ■

Spangle Swallowtail ■ *Papilio protenor* 藍鳳蝶 WS 105–115mm

DESCRIPTION Both male and female resemble male Great Mormon Swallowtail (opposite) but have longer hindwing. Less red on hindwing, and no red on wing-base below. Sexes similar. **DISTRIBUTION** Common in HKI, NT and Lantau. Otherwise found from India to central and southern China, through mainland SE Asia and Korea. **HABITAT AND HABITS** Occurs in lowland woodland and citrus orchards; less likely to be seen in parks than Great Mormon, and flight slower. Adults sip nectar, and male often seen puddling. Caterpillars feed on Mandarin *Citrus reticulata*, Kumquat C. (*Fortunella*) *japonica*, Wampi *Clausena lansium*, Shiny-leaved Prickly Ash *Zanthoxylum nitidum*, Big-leaved Prickly Ash *Z. myriacanthum* and Climbing Prickly Ash *Z. scandens* in citrus (Rutaceae) family. Seen Mar–Dec.

Chinese Peacock Swallowtail ■ *Papilio bianor* 碧鳳蝶 WS 90–120mm

DESCRIPTION Large black swallowtail with metallic blue and green scales. Both sexes have red marginal hindwing-spots below, and large wing-tail. Female also has red hindwing-spots above. Quite similar to Southern Chinese Peacock Swallowtail (p. 24), but tail margins matte black, lack metallic scales and often have matte black band without metallic scales above. Also, on forewing-underside, in the present species metallic scales cover 50 per cent of wing from base, v 30 per cent or less in Southern Chinese. **DISTRIBUTION** Uncommon in HKI and NT; fairly common in Lantau. Otherwise found from India, to northern China and the Korean Peninsula, through mainland SE Asia. **HABITAT AND HABITS** Occurs in wooded areas. Flight slow and heavy. Adults sip nectar and visit wet mud. Caterpillars feed on *Tetradium* (*Euodia*) *glabrifolium* in citrus (Rutaceae) family. Seen Apr–Sep.

▪ Papilionidae ▪

Southern Chinese Peacock Swallowtail ▪ *Papilio dialis*
穹翠鳳蝶 WS 100–120mm

DESCRIPTION Large black swallowtail with metallic blue and green scales. Quite similar to Chinese Peacock Swallowtail (p. 23), but present species has metallic scales at tail margins. **DISTRIBUTION** Uncommon in HKI, NT and Lantau. Global range restricted to southern China. **HABITAT AND HABITS** Occurs in wooded areas. Flight slow and heavy. Adults sip nectar and visit wet mud. Caterpillars feed on plants in citrus (Rutaceae) family, including Orange Climber *Zanthoxylum* (*Toddalia*) *asiatica*. Seen Apr–Oct.

Paris Peacock Swallowtail ▪ *Papilio paris* 巴黎翠鳳蝶 WS 85–105mm

DESCRIPTION Beautiful metallic green scaling, with distinctive blue or green patch on hindwing, make this butterfly identifiable at a distance. Wing-tail present, and sexes similar. **DISTRIBUTION** Common in HKI, NT and Lantau. Otherwise found from India to southern China, through mainland SE Asia. **HABITAT AND HABITS** Occurs in wooded areas, mainly at low elevations. Flight strong. Adults sip nectar, and males may visit wet mud. Caterpillars feed on Thin Evodia *Melicope* (*Euodia*) *pteleifolia* (*lepta*), Orange Climber *Zanthoxylum* (*Toddalia*) *asiatica* and Prickly Ash *Z. avicennae* in citrus (Rutaceae) family. Seen year round, with peak Mar–June and again in Nov.

■ PAPILIONIDAE ■

Red Helen Swallowtail ■ *Papilio helenus* 玉斑鳳蝶 WS 90–110mm

DESCRIPTION Distinctive white hindwing-patches visible in flight but often hidden at rest. Otherwise black, with red hindwing spotting below, and wing-tail. Sexes similar. May be confused with the Common Rose Swallowtail (p. 18) above but lacks pink body and white hindwing-patches in different location. **DISTRIBUTION** Common in HKI, NT and Lantau. Otherwise found from India, to central and southern China, through mainland SE Asia, to Borneo, the Philippines and Japan.

HABITAT AND HABITS Occurs in wooded areas, citrus orchards and parks. Flight strong. Adults sip nectar, and males visit wet mud. Caterpillars feed on Sweet Orange *Citrus* x *sinensis*, Kumquat *C.* (*Fortunella*) *japonica* and *hindsii*, Wampi *Clausena lansium*, Flower Axistree *Glycosmis parviflora*, *Tetradium* (*Euodia*) *glabrifolium*, Orange Climber *Zanthoxylum* (*Toddalia*) *asiatica*, Shiny-leaved Prickly Ash *Z. nitidum*, Big-leaved Prickly Ash *Z. myriacanthum*, Prickly Ash *Z. avicennae* and Climbing Prickly Ash *Z. scandens* in citrus (Rutaceae) family, and *Rhus hypoleuca* in cashew (Anacardiaceae) family. Seen Mar–Dec.

25

◼ Papilionidae ◼

Lime Swallowtail ◼ *Papilio demoleus* 達摩鳳蝶 WS 80–90mm

DESCRIPTION Black with creamy white patches. Red (and even blue) hindwing-spots, and no wing-tail. Sexes similar. **DISTRIBUTION** Fairly common in HKI, NT and Lantau. Otherwise broadly distributed from the Middle East, to China, South and SE Asia, to eastern Indonesia and Australia. Introduced to the Caribbean. **HABITAT AND HABITS** Occurs in open woodland and shrubland, including on small islands. Flight swift, near the ground. Adults sip nectar. Caterpillars feed on plants in citrus (Rutaceae) family, including Lemon *Citrus* x *limon*, Kumquat *C*. (*Fortunella*) *japonica* and *hindsii*, Wampi *Clausena lansium*, Flower Axistree *Glycosmis parviflora* and especially Chinese Box-Orange *Severinia* (*Atalantia*) *buxifolia*. Seen Feb–Dec.

Chinese Yellow Swallowtail ◼ *Papilio xuthus* 柑橘鳳蝶 WS 80–110mm

DESCRIPTION Pale yellow with black stripes and wing-tail. Orange and blue spotting below on hindwing. Female darker than male, but sexes similar. **DISTRIBUTION** Fairly common in HKI and NT; rare in Lantau. Otherwise broadly distributed north to central and northern China, south-east Siberia, Korea and Japan. **HABITAT AND HABITS** Occurs in open woodland and secondary scrub, often at high elevations. Flight slower than in many swallowtails. Adults sip nectar, and males may hilltop. Caterpillars feed on Shiny-leaved Prickly Ash *Zanthoxylum nitidum* and Big-leaved Prickly Ash *Z. myriacanthum* in citrus (Rutaceae) family. Seen Jan–Apr, July–Dec, and especially Oct–Nov.

HESPERIIDAE

Indian Awlking *Choaspes benjaminii* 綠弄蝶 WS 45–50mm

DESCRIPTION Medium-sized skipper. Grey-purple above. Yellowish with charcoal veins below, with bright orange and black tornus. Very similar to Orange Red Skirt (p. 28), but Indian Awlking generally has yellow suffusion across forewing and hindwing (v mainly hindwing in Orange Red Skirt). Put differently, from underneath the Indian Awlking has similar colouration in forewing and hindwing, while Orange Red Skirt has duller forewing than hindwing. Also, from above, this species fairly even blue across forewing, while Orange Red Skirt has contrast between greenish inner half and blue outer half of wing. Caterpillars strikingly different: black with bold yellow bands in this species, and black with yellow spotting in Orange Red Skirt. Sexes similar. **DISTRIBUTION** Rarely identified in HK due to confusion between this species and Orange Red Skirt. Not seen in HKI and Lantau; rare in NT. Otherwise found from India to central and southern China, Korea and Japan, through mainland SE Asia. **HABITAT AND HABITS** Occurs in wooded areas. At dusk flies quickly on regular circuit along streams and trails. By day, rests on undersides of leaves with wings held vertically. Adults sip nectar. Caterpillars feed on Stiff-leaved Meliosma *Meliosma ridgida* and Ford's Meliosma *M. fordii* in sabia (Sabiaceae) family. Adults seen Mar–Dec.

HESPERIIDAE

Orange Red Skirt ■ *Choaspes hemixanthus* 半黃綠弄蝶 WS 45–50mm

DESCRIPTION Medium-sized skipper. Grey-green above. Yellowish with charcoal veins below, with bright orange and black tornus. Very similar to Indian Awlking (p. 27), but this species generally has yellow suffusion across both forewing and hindwing (v mainly hindwing in Orange Red Skirt). Caterpillars strikingly different, black with yellow spotting in this species, and black with bold yellow bands in Indian Awlking. Sexes similar.
DISTRIBUTION Rarely identified in HK due to confusion between species mentioned above. Rare in HKI and NT; not seen in Lantau. Otherwise found from India to central and southern China, Korea and Japan, through mainland SE Asia. **HABITAT AND HABITS** Found in wooded areas, often at higher elevation than Indian Awlking. At dusk flies quickly on regular circuit along streams and trails. By day, rests on undersides of leaves with wings held vertically. Adults sip nectar. Caterpillars feed on *Sabia limoniacea* plants in sabia (Sabiaceae) family. Adults seen Mar–Nov.

■ HESPERIIDAE ■

Pale Green Awlet ■ *Bibasis (Burara) gomata* 白傘弄蝶 WS 40–45mm

DESCRIPTION Medium-sized skipper. Above brown (male) or metallic blue (female). Black below with white radiating lines. Body orange. **DISTRIBUTION** Uncommonly seen overall. Fairly common in HKI; uncommon in NT and Lantau. Otherwise found from India to southern China, through mainland SE Asia, to Borneo and the Philippines. **HABITAT AND HABITS** Occurs in wooded areas and secondary growth. Not active by day, but can be seen at dawn or (especially) dusk. At dusk flies quickly in woodland clearings or along paths. Rests with wings held vertically. Adults sip nectar. Caterpillars feed on Ivy Tree *Heptapleurum* (*Schefflera*) *heptaphyllum* plants in ivy (Araliaceae) family. Adults seen Feb–Mar, June–July and Oct–Dec.

Male    *Female*

Branded Orange Awlet ■ *Bibasis (Burara) oedipodea* 黑斑傘弄蝶
WS 40–45mm

DESCRIPTION Medium-sized skipper. Body orange. Above sooty-black with long blue hairs at base. Below brownish-orange with orange (male) or bright orange (female) hindwing-margin. **DISTRIBUTION** Uncommon in HKI, NT and Lantau. Otherwise found from India to southern China, through mainland SE Asia and the Philippines. **HABITAT AND HABITS** Occurs in wooded areas. Only active during cloudy days or at dawn and dusk. Very wary, with fast flight. Rests with wings held vertically. Adults sip nectar, especially from *Vitex* flowers. Caterpillars feed on Hiptage *Hiptage benghalensis* in malpighias (Malpighiaceae) family. Adults seen Mar–June and Aug–Nov.

■ HESPERIIDAE ■

Brown Awl ■ *Badamia exclamationis* 尖翅弄蝶 WS 45–55mm

DESCRIPTION Medium to large skipper. Wings plain brown. Forewing longer and narrower than in other skippers. Female can have some spotting, reduced in male. Narrow yellow abdominal banding, with orange antennae tips. **DISTRIBUTION** Rare in HK Island, New Territories and Lantau. Otherwise found from India to southern China, through mainland SE Asia, to the Philippines, Australia, the Mariana Islands and east to Fiji. **HABITAT AND HABITS** Occurs in wooded areas. Active by day. Migratory, which is unusual in a skipper. Fast and erratic flight. Rests with wings held vertically. Adults sip nectar. Caterpillars feed on Hiptage *Hiptage benghalensis* in malpighias (Malpighiaceae) family. Adults seen Apr–Aug.

Common Awl ■ *Hasora badra* 三斑趾弄蝶 WS 40–45mm

DESCRIPTION Medium-sized skipper. Wings brown with slight purplish sheen below. HK hosts two species of *Hasora* skipper lacking white stripes and having two spots below on hindwing: Common Awl and Slate Awl (opposite). Common has 'bump' (tornal lobe) protruding from hindwing; also often dark spot next to this lobe. Slate has more rounded wings, and typically lacks both these field marks. Plain brown above (male) or three square hyaline spots in centre and three beige subapical spots near tip (female). **DISTRIBUTION** Rare in HKI and Lantau; fairly common in NT. Otherwise found from India to southern China, through mainland SE Asia, to Borneo. **HABITAT AND HABITS** The most commonly seen *Hasora* skipper in HK. Occurs in wooded areas and secondary growth. Typically seen late in day, near dusk. Flight fast and often rests, with wings held vertically, on undersides of leaves. Adults sip nectar, especially from *Lantana* flowers. Caterpillars feed on White-flowered Derris *Derris alborubra* and Thick-pericarped Millettia *Millettia pachycarpa* in legume (Fabaceae) family. Adults seen June–July and Sep–Jan.

Male

Female

HESPERIIDAE

Slate Awl — *Hasora anuraa* 無趾弄蝶 WS 40–45mm

DESCRIPTION Medium-sized brown skipper. Unlike Common Awl (opposite), Slate has more rounded wings without protruding tornal lobe on hindwing. Also, this area of hindwing typically lighter in Slate. Above plain brown (male) or with three square hyaline spots in centre and three beige subapical spots near tip (female). **DISTRIBUTION** Not seen in HKI or Lantau; rare in NT. Otherwise found from India to southern China. **HABITAT AND HABITS** Occurs in wooded areas and secondary growth. Typically seen late in day, near dusk. Flight fast and often rests, with wings held vertically, on undersides of leaves. Adults sip nectar. Caterpillars feed on Glittering-leaved Callerya *Callerya* (*Millettia*) *nitida* and Diel's Callerya *C.* (*Millettia*) *dielsiana* in legume (Fabaceae) family. Adults seen Feb–Oct.

Common Banded Awl — *Hasora chromus* 雙斑趾弄蝶 WS 40–45mm

DESCRIPTION Medium-sized brown skipper. Hong Kong hosts three species of *Hasora* skipper with clear white hindwing-stripe below: Common Banded, Plain Banded and White Banded Awls (p.32). Common typically has medium-sized white band and plain brown wings, lacking metallic sheen of other two species (though present species sometimes shows slight violet sheen). Hindwing protrudes in bottom corner, the tornal lobe. Forewing plain brown in male; female has two hyaline spots in centre. **DISTRIBUTION** Uncommon in HKI, NT and Lantau. Otherwise found from India to southern China, through mainland SE Asia, the Philippines, Indonesia, and Australia to Samoa. **HABITAT AND HABITS** Occurs in wooded areas near coast. More often seen by day than other *Hasora* skippers and not as often seen resting on undersides of leaves. Flight fast. Rests with wings held vertically. Adults sip nectar. Caterpillars feed on Indian Beech Tree *Pongamia* (*Millettia*) *pinnata* in legume (Fabaceae) family. Adults seen Apr–Nov, especially Apr–July.

■ HESPERIIDAE ■

Plain Banded Awl ■ *Hasora vitta* 緯帶趾弄蝶 WS 40–45mm

DESCRIPTION Medium-sized brown skipper. Compared to other two *Hasora* species, often has wider white band below and single subapical spot near forewing-tip. More gloss below than in Common Banded Awl (p. 31). Hindwing protrudes in bottom corner, the tornal lobe. Above plain brown (male), or with two hyaline spots in centre (female).
DISTRIBUTION Rare in HKI and NT; not seen in Lantau. Otherwise found from India to southern China, through mainland SE Asia, to Borneo. HABITAT AND HABITS Occurs in wooded areas at higher elevations. Fairly visible by day. Flight fast and often rests on undersides of leaves, with wings held vertically. Adults sip nectar. Caterpillars feed on Glittering-leaved Callerya *Callerya* (*Millettia*) *nitida* and Diel's Callerya *C.* (*Millettia*) *dielsiana* in legume (Fabaceae) family. Adults seen Apr–Oct.

Fresh    *Worn*

White Banded Awl ■ *Hasora taminatus* 銀針趾弄蝶 WS 40–45mm

DESCRIPTION Medium-sized skipper. Wings brown. Compared to the other two banded awls (p. 31 and above), often has narrower white band below and no subapical spot near forewing tip. More gloss below than in Common, which may extend in front and behind white stripe. Hindwing protrudes in bottom corner, the tornal lobe. Above plain brown (male), or with two small spots in centre (female). DISTRIBUTION Rare in HKI; not seen in NT and Lantau. Otherwise found from India to southern China, through mainland SE Asia, to Borneo and the Philippines. HABITAT AND HABITS Occurs in wooded areas. Fairly visible by day. Flight fast and often rests on undersides of leaves, with wings held vertically. Adults sip nectar. Caterpillars feed on *Callerya* (*Millettia*) plants in legume (Fabaceae) family. Adults seen May–July, especially May.

■ HESPERIIDAE ■

Water Snow Flat ■ *Tagiades litigiosa* 沾邊裙弄蝶 WS 40mm

DESCRIPTION Medium-sized skipper that holds wings flat at rest. Wings dark brown. Distal half of hindwing white, with four brown spots along trailing edge. Sexes similar. DISTRIBUTION Fairly common in HKI, NT and Lantau. Otherwise found from India to southern China, through mainland SE Asia and western Indonesia. HABITAT AND HABITS Occurs in lowland wooded areas, often along streams. Flight rapid. Active by day. Rests on undersides of leaves with wings held flat, possibly to avoid detection by predators. Adults sip nectar, especially from *Vitex negundo*. Caterpillars feed on Shoulang Yam *Dioscorea cirrhosa* and Ford's Yam *D. fordii* in true yam (Dioscoreaceae) family. Adults seen Apr–Nov.

Dark-edged Snow Flat ■ *Tagiades menaka* 黑邊裙弄蝶 WS 40mm

DESCRIPTION Medium-sized skipper that holds wings flat at rest. Wings dark brown. Distal half of hindwing white, with large brown spots along trailing edge that form thick band, and one brown spot in large white patch. Sexes similar. DISTRIBUTION Uncommon in HKI and NT; rare in Lantau. Otherwise found from India to southern China, through mainland SE Asia and western Indonesia. HABITAT AND HABITS Occurs in lowland wooded areas. Flight rapid. Active by day. Rests on undersides of leaves with wings held flat, possibly to avoid detection by predators. Adults sip nectar, especially from *Vitex negundo*. Caterpillar host plant not well known, but in India recently reported on Air Potato *Dioscorea bulbifera* in true yam (Dioscoreaceae) family. Adults seen Apr–Nov.

■ HESPERIIDAE ■

White-banded Flat ■ *Gerosis phisara* 匪夷捷弄蝶 WS 40mm

DESCRIPTION Distinctive medium-sized skipper that holds wings flat at rest. Wings brown with three square white forewing-spots. White band that curves from forewing to hindwing. Width of band variable, though usually wider in dry-season form. Head tawny-brown. Sexes similar. **DISTRIBUTION** Uncommon. Not seen in HKI and Lantau; fairly common in NT. Otherwise found from India to southern China, through mainland SE Asia. **HABITAT AND HABITS** Occurs in wooded areas. Flight rapid. Active by day. Adults sip nectar. Caterpillars feed on Bentham's Rosewood *Dalbergia benthamii* in legume (Fabaceae) family. Adults seen Mar–Oct.

Magpie Flat ■ *Abraximorpha davidii* 白弄蝶 WS 45–55mm

DESCRIPTION Striking skipper that holds its wings flat at rest. Unlike any other butterfly in HK, though may be mistaken for a moth. Head and thorax orange, and wings white with medium-sized dark grey spots. Sexes similar. **DISTRIBUTION** Uncommon overall. Not seen in HKI or Lantau; fairly common in NT. Otherwise only found in central and southeastern China. **HABITAT AND HABITS** Occurs in wooded areas, especially around Tai Mo Shan. Flight rapid. Active by day. Adults sip nectar. Caterpillars feed on Rusty-haired Raspberry *Rubus reflexus* in rose (Rosaceae) family and Chinese Bittersweet *Celastrus hindsii* in staff vine (Celastraceae) family. Adults seen May–Aug.

HESPERIIDAE

Chestnut Banded Angle ■ *Odontoptilum angulata* 角翅弄蝶 WS 40–45mm

DESCRIPTION Medium-sized, camouflaged skipper. Wings brown, black and white, with wavy margin. Sexes similar. **DISTRIBUTION** Uncommon overall. Uncommon in HKI and NT; fairly common in Lantau. Otherwise found from India to southern China, through mainland SE Asia and western Indonesia. **HABITAT AND HABITS** Occurs in wooded areas in lowlands. Flight rapid, and active in sunshine. Adults sip nectar, especially *Lantana* and *Vitex*. Rests on uppersides of leaves with wings held flat. Caterpillars feed on the common lowland edge tree *Grewia* (*Microcos*) *nervosa* (*paniculata*) and seashore- and mangrove-associated tree Cuban Bast *Hibiscus tiliaceus*, both in mallow (Malvaceae) family. Adults seen Apr–Oct.

Yellow-spotted Angle ■ *Caprona alida* 白彩弄蝶 WS 35mm

DESCRIPTION Medium-sized skipper with irregular wing-margins. Wet-season form greyish-brown above with white and tan spots; underside white with black spots. Dry-season form plainer, with fewer spots above and plain underside. Sexes similar. **DISTRIBUTION** Uncommon. Not seen in HKI; uncommon in NT and Lantau. Otherwise found from India to southern China, through mainland SE Asia and western Indonesia. **HABITAT AND HABITS** Found in scrub and grassland, where male can be territorial. Flight rapid. Active by day. Adults sip nectar. Rests with wings held flat. Caterpillars feed on *Helicteres* plants in mallow (Malvaceae) family. Adults seen Mar–Aug.

Wet-season form    *Dry-season form*

▪ HESPERIIDAE ▪

Common Spotted Flat ▪ *Celaenorrhinus leucocera* 白角星弄蝶 WS 45mm

DESCRIPTION Medium-sized skipper. Wings brown with white band in middle of forewing. Hindwing marked with around 10 yellow spots. Sexes similar. **DISTRIBUTION** Rare overall. Rare in HKI and NT; not seen in Lantau. Otherwise found from India to southern China, through mainland SE Asia. **HABITAT AND HABITS** Occurs in wooded areas. Flight rapid and low to the ground. Active by day. Rests with wings held flat. Adults sip nectar. Caterpillars feed on Blue Eranthemum *Eranthemum pulchellum* (*nervosum*) in acanthus (Acanthaceae) family. Adults seen Apr–Dec.

Common Bush Hopper ▪ *Ampittia dioscorides* 黃斑弄蝶 WS 20mm

DESCRIPTION Smallest HK skipper. Brown wings with orange patches, more developed in male than female. Hindwing-underside orange with dark markings that are shorter and rounder than in Striped Bush Hopper (opposite). **DISTRIBUTION** Uncommon. Not seen in HKI; uncommon in NT and Lantau. Otherwise found from India to central and southern China, through mainland SE Asia and western Indonesia. **HABITAT AND HABITS** Occurs in marshy grassland and abandoned paddy fields. Flight rapid and brief, close to the ground. Active by day. Adults sip nectar, especially of *Lantana* and *Vitex*. Caterpillars feed on Asian Rice *Oryza sativa* and Native Rice Grass *Leersia hexandra* in grass (Poaceae) family. Adults seen Mar–Nov, especially Oct–Nov.

Male   *Female*

◾ HESPERIIDAE ◾

Striped Bush Hopper ◾ *Ampittia virgata* 鉤形黃斑弄蝶 WS 25mm

DESCRIPTION Small skipper, slightly larger than Common Bush Hopper (opposite). Localized in HK. Similar to Common, with brown wings and orange markings. Hindwing-underside orange with longer dark markings than in Common. **DISTRIBUTION** Uncommon. Not seen in HKI and NT; uncommon in Lantau. Otherwise restricted to southeastern China. **HABITAT AND HABITS** Occurs in hillside grassland, especially around Ngong Ping. Flight rapid and brief, close to the ground. Active by day. Adults sip nectar, especially of *Lantana* and *Vitex*. Caterpillar host plant not well known, but probably in grass (Poaceae) family. Adults seen May–Sep.

Grey Scrub Hopper ◾ *Aeromachus jhora* 寬鍔弄蝶 WS 20–25mm

DESCRIPTION Small, dark brown skipper with diffuse light and brown markings, often forming faint vertical line on hindwing underside (missing in Pygmy Scrub Hopper, p. 38). Very similar to Pygmy, but generally browner. **DISTRIBUTION** Fairly recent addition to HK butterfly fauna. Generally uncommon. Not seen in HKI; uncommon in NT; rare in Lantau. Otherwise found from India to southern China, through mainland SE Asia. **HABITAT AND HABITS** Active by day. Wings held vertically at rest. Adults sip nectar. Caterpillar host plant not well known, but probably in grass (Poaceae) family. Adults seen year round.

◾ HESPERIIDAE ◾

Pygmy Scrub Hopper ◾ *Aeromachus pygmaeus* 侏儒鍔弄蝶 WS 20mm

DESCRIPTION Very small skipper, dark greyish-brown with no clear patterning, unlike Grey Scrub Hopper (p. 37), which often has faint vertical line on hindwing-underside. Very similar to Grey, but generally greyer. **DISTRIBUTION** Rare. Not seen in HKI and Lantau; rare in NT. Otherwise found from India to central and southern China, through mainland SE Asia and the Philippines. **HABITAT AND HABITS** Found in marshy grassland and abandoned paddy fields. Flight rapid and brief, close to the ground. Active by day. Adults sip nectar. Caterpillars known to feed on Saint Augustine Grass *Stenotaphrum secundatum* and *Polytrias indica* in grass (Poaceae) family. Adults seen year round.

Moore's Ace ◾ *Halpe porus* 雙子酣弄蝶 WS 35–40mm

DESCRIPTION Medium-sized skipper. Brown wings with light hyaline patches. Basal areas of hindwing-underside can be tawny. Sexes similar. **DISTRIBUTION** Rare. Not seen in HKI and Lantau; rare in NT. Otherwise found from India to southern China, through mainland SE Asia. **HABITAT AND HABITS** Found in open country near bamboo. Flight rapid, with adults often chasing each other near ridges. Active by day. Adults sip nectar. Caterpillars feed on *Bambusa* plants in grass (Poaceae) family. Adults seen Apr–Oct.

▪ HESPERIIDAE ▪

Monastyrskyi's Ace ▪ *Thoressa monastyrskyi* 黑斑陀弄蝶 WS 35–40mm

DESCRIPTION Medium-sized skipper. Dark brown above with several light hyaline patches, plus yellow on hindwing. Orange below with dark submarginal spotting. Females have less orange below than males. **DISTRIBUTION** Rare since first recorded around 2002. Not seen in HKI and Lantau; rare and only in east in NT. Otherwise only known from northern Vietnam. **HABITAT AND HABITS** Found in uplands near bamboo, with some hilltopping behaviour. Adults occasionally visit flowers, and caterpillars feed on bamboo in grass (Poaceae) family. Adults only seen in narrow timeframe, in mid-May–early June.

Male    *Male*    *Female*

Tree Flitter ▪ *Hyarotis adrastus* 希弄蝶 WS 35–40mm

DESCRIPTION Medium-sized skipper. Dark brown above with several light hyaline patches. Mixed pattern below of dark brown, tawny and white. Sexes similar. **DISTRIBUTION** Uncommon. Fairly common in HKI; uncommon in NT; rare in Lantau. Otherwise found from India to southern China, through mainland SE Asia, to western Indonesia. **HABITAT AND HABITS** Occurs at a variety of elevations near host plants. Adults do not fly a great deal, often returning to favoured perch. Active by day. Rarely seen sipping nectar. Caterpillars feed on Four-finger Rattan Palm *Calamus tetradactylus* and Spiny Date Palm *Phoenix loureiroi* (*hanceana*), as well as cultivated palms like Pygmy Date Palm *P. roebelenii* and Areca Palm *Dypsis* (*Chrysalidocarpus*) *lutescens* in palm (Arecaceae) family. Adults seen Mar–Oct.

HESPERIIDAE

Indian Palm Bob ■ *Suastus gremius* 素弄蝶 WS 30mm

DESCRIPTION Small skipper. Dark brown wings with several white spots above. Black spots below on hindwing unique to this species. Sexes similar. **DISTRIBUTION** Fairly common in HKI and NT; uncommon in Lantau. Otherwise found from India to southern China, through mainland SE Asia, the Philippines, Borneo and western Indonesia. **HABITAT AND HABITS** Occurs in urban areas, as well as scrubby spots near host plants. Flight strong and brief. Active by day. Adults sip nectar. Caterpillars feed on Spiny Date Palm *Phoenix loureiroi* (*hanceana*) and Lady Palm *Rhapis excelsa*, as well as cultivated palms like Pygmy Date Palm *Phoenix roebelenii* in palm (Arecaceae) family. Adults seen Feb–Dec.

Purple and Gold Flitter ■ *Zographetus satwa* 黃裳腫脈弄蝶 WS 30–35mm

DESCRIPTION Small skipper. Distinctive: front half yellow with three purplish-brown dots. Rear half broadly purplish-brown. Sexes similar. **DISTRIBUTION** Uncommon overall. Uncommon in HKI, NT and Lantau. Otherwise found from India to southern China, through mainland SE Asia. **HABITAT AND HABITS** Occurs in shrubland and agricultural areas. Flight strong. Active by day. Caterpillars feed on Champion's Bauhinia *Phanera* (*Bauhinia*) *championii* in legume (Fabaceae) family. Adults seen Apr–Dec.

▪ Hesperiidae ▪

Shiny-spotted Bob ▪ *Isoteinon lamprospilus* 旖弄蝶 WS 30mm

DESCRIPTION Small skipper. Brown wings, highlighted with auburn below. Below on hindwing, 8–10 dark-rimmed white spots. Sexes similar. **DISTRIBUTION** Rare. Not seen in HKI and Lantau; rare in NT, mainly in Plover Cove. Otherwise found in eastern China, Korea and Japan. **HABITAT AND HABITS** Occurs in wooded areas of northern NT. Flight strong and brief. Active by day. Adults sip nectar. Caterpillars feed on Chinese Silvergrass *Miscanthus sinensis* in grass (Poaceae) family. Adults seen Apr–Sep.

Common Redeye ▪ *Matapa aria* 瑪弄蝶 WS 40mm

DESCRIPTION Medium-sized skipper. Eyes red. Wings plain reddish-brown. Sexes similar. **DISTRIBUTION** Uncommon overall. Uncommon in HKI Island and NT; rare in Lantau. Otherwise found from India to southern China, through mainland SE Asia, the Philippines and western Indonesia. **HABITAT AND HABITS** Found near bamboo groves. Flight strong. Can occasionally be seen feeding by day, including in sunny weather, but often found resting at this time. Most active at dusk and dawn, and by night, when it is attracted to lights. Adults sip nectar. Caterpillars feed on *Bambusa*, *Schizostachyum* and *Phyllostachys* bamboo in grass (Poaceae) family. Adults seen Mar–Nov, especially Sep–Nov.

■ HESPERIIDAE ■

Rounded Palm-Redeye ■ *Erionota torus* 黃斑蕉弄蝶 WS 65–75mm

DESCRIPTION Very large skipper, the largest in HK. Eyes red. Wings brown, with three yellow forewing-spots. Sexes similar. **DISTRIBUTION** Uncommon overall. Uncommon in HKI, NT and Lantau. Otherwise found from India to southern China, through mainland SE Asia, the Philippines, Borneo and western Indonesia. **HABITAT AND HABITS** Occurs in cultivated areas near host plant. Flight strong. Active at dusk and dawn, and probably by night. Adults sip nectar, especially from banana flowers. Caterpillars feed on Banana *Musa* x *paradisiaca* in banana (Musaceae) family. Adults seen Apr–Oct.

Restricted Demon ■ *Notocrypta curvifascia* 曲紋袖弄蝶 WS 40mm

DESCRIPTION Medium-sized skipper. Blackish wings with diagonal white band and several small white apical spots, distinguishing it from Common Banded Demon (opposite). Sexes similar. **DISTRIBUTION** Uncommon. Fairly common in HKI; uncommon in NT; rare in Lantau. Otherwise found from India, to central and southern China, Japan, mainland SE Asia, Borneo and western Indonesia. **HABITAT AND HABITS** Occurs in woodland. Flight fairly strong and far ranging for a skipper. Active by day. Adults feed on bird droppings and seldom visit flowers. Caterpillars feed on *Alpinia* and White Ginger Lily *Hedychium coronarium* plants in ginger (Zingiberaceae) family. Adults seen Mar–Nov.

▪ HESPERIIDAE ▪

Common Banded Demon ▪ *Notocrypta paralysos* 窄紋袖弄蝶 WS 35–40mm

DESCRIPTION Small to medium skipper. Blackish wings with diagonal white band. Differs from Restricted Demon (opposite) by having zero (maximum one) white apical spots. Sexes similar. **DISTRIBUTION** Uncommon. Fairly common in HKI; uncommon in NT; rare in Lantau. Otherwise found from India to southern China, through mainland SE Asia, the Philippines, Borneo and western Indonesia. **HABITAT AND HABITS** Occurs in woodland. Flight fairly strong and far ranging for a skipper. Active by day. Adults feed on bird droppings and seldom visit flowers. Caterpillars feed on True Ginger *Zingiber*, Spiral Ginger *Costus* and Turmeric *Curcuma* plants in ginger (Zingiberaceae) family. Adults seen Feb–Dec.

Grass Demon ▪ *Udaspes folus* 薑弄蝶 WS 40–50mm

DESCRIPTION Medium to large skipper. Dark brown wings with several white spots above, and one large white spot below on hindwing. Sexes similar. **DISTRIBUTION** Uncommon overall. Uncommon in HKI, NT and Lantau. Otherwise found from India to southern China, through mainland SE Asia, Borneo and western Indonesia. **HABITAT AND HABITS** Occurs in cultivated areas or secondary woodland. Flight fairly strong. Active by day. Adults sip nectar. Caterpillars feed on Ginger *Zingiber officinale* and White Ginger Lily *Hedychium coronarium* in ginger (Zingiberaceae) family. Adults seen Mar–Oct.

▪ Hesperiidae ▪

Chestnut Bob ▪ *Iambrix salsala* 雅弄蝶 WS 30mm

DESCRIPTION Small skipper. Orange-brown wings, with three medium-sized white spots below on hindwing. Spots rimmed with dark brown. Female has more light spots on forewing, but otherwise sexes similar. **DISTRIBUTION** Uncommon overall. Uncommon in HKI and Lantau; fairly common in NT. Otherwise found from India to southern China, through mainland SE Asia, to western Indonesia. **HABITAT AND HABITS** Occurs in grassy areas adjacent to woodland. Flight short and swift. Active by day, when adults sip nectar. Caterpillars feed on Sasagrass *Lophatherum gracile* in grass (Poaceae) family. Adults seen Apr–Oct, especially June.

Forest Hopper ▪ *Astictopterus jama* 腌翅弄蝶 WS 30–35mm

DESCRIPTION Small skipper. Round wings dark brown and plain. Female has small light spots near forewing-tip, but otherwise sexes similar. **DISTRIBUTION** Fairly common overall. Fairly common in HKI and NT; uncommon in Lantau. Otherwise found from India to southern China, through mainland SE Asia, to western Indonesia. **HABITAT AND HABITS** Often seen in hillside grassland, where it flies slowly for short distances. Active by day; rarely seen sipping nectar. Caterpillars feed on grasses, including common hillside silvergrasses *Miscanthus floridulus* and *M. sinensis*, as well as *Digitaria* and Burma Reed *Neyraudia reynaudiana* in grass (Poaccac) family. Adults seen Mar–Oct.

HESPERIIDAE

Identification of male palm darts		Forewing streaks reach termen	Brand present	Brand centred
Plain Palm Dart	Cephrenes acalle	No	No	-
Dark Palm Dart	Telicota ohara	No	Yes	Yes, narrow
Hainan Palm Dart	Telicota besta	No	Yes	No
Greenish Palm Dart	Telicota bambusae	Yes	Yes	Yes, wide
Pale Palm Dart	Telicota colon	Yes	Yes	No

Female palm darts often unidentifiable to species level in the field. Males may be identified by close inspection of 1. the termen and 2. the brand (is brand present, and if so, is it centered in the darker brown streak?), as summarized in the table above.

Male brand

Orange streaks do not reach the wing margin (termen).

Plain Palm Dart ■ *Cephrenes acalle* 金斑弄蝶 WS 45mm

DESCRIPTION Medium-sized skipper. Wings dark brown and orange. Similar to *Telicota* palm darts, but forewing upperside lacks brand in the brown streak, orange streaks do not reach wing-edge (termen), plus additional orange line on inner part of forewing next to body. **DISTRIBUTION** Uncommonly identified in HK. Fairly common in HKI; rare in NT and Lantau. Otherwise found from southern to northern China, Korea and Japan. **HABITAT AND HABITS** Flight darting and fast. Most active at dawn and dusk, with wings held half open at rest. Adults sip nectar. Caterpillars feed on Chinese Fan Palm *Livistona chinensis* and Coconut Palm *Cocos nucifera* in palm (Arecaceae) family. Adults seen year round, less often in winter.

▪ HESPERIIDAE ▪

Dark Palm Dart ▪ *Telicota ohara* 黃紋長標弄蝶 WS 35mm

DESCRIPTION Medium-sized skipper. Wings dark brown and orange. Can be difficult to distinguish from other *Telicota* skippers, with female sometimes indistinguishable in the field. Useful field marks for male include: on forewing upperside, wing edge dark brown and orange streaks do not reach termen (unlike in Greenish and Pale Palm Darts, p. 48); on forewing upperside, male 'brand' centrally placed in brown streak (unlike in Hainan Palm Dart, opposite). Brand narrow. Sexes similar, though female lacks forewing brand. **DISTRIBUTION** Rarely identified in HK. Not seen in HKI and Lantau; rare in NT. Otherwise found from India to southern China, through mainland SE Asia, to western Indonesia, Borneo and the Philippines. **HABITAT AND HABITS** Occurs in abandoned agricultural areas, gardens and secondary growth. Flight darting and fast. Active by day, with wings held half open at rest on flowers and grass. Often territorial, chasing others away before returning to rest. Adults sip nectar. Caterpillars feed on grasses, including Palmgrass *Setaria palmifolia*, Pacific Island Silvergrass *Miscanthus floridulus* and Chinese Silvergrass *M. sinensis* in grass (Poaceae) family. Adults seen Mar–Dec.

▪ Hesperiidae ▪

Hainan Palm Dart ▪ *Telicota besta* 黑脈長標弄蝶 WS 35–40mm

DESCRIPTION Medium-sized skipper. Wings dark brown and orange. Can be difficult to distinguish from other *Telicota* skippers, with female sometimes indistinguishable in the field. Useful field marks for male include: on forewing upperside, wing edge dark brown, and orange streaks do not reach termen (unlike in Greenish and Pale Palm Darts, p. 48); on forewing upperside, male 'brand' not centrally placed in brown streak, but rather off centre (unlike Dark Palm Dart, opposite). Sexes similar, though female does not have forewing brand. **DISTRIBUTION** Rarely identified in HK. Rare in HKI and NT; not seen in Lantau. Otherwise found from India to southern China, through mainland SE Asia, to western Indonesia, Borneo and the Philippines. **HABITAT AND HABITS** Occurs in abandoned agricultural areas, gardens and secondary growth. Flight darting and fast. Active by day, with wings held half open at rest on flowers and grass. Often territorial, chasing others away before returning to rest. Adults sip nectar. Caterpillars feed on Chinese Silvergrass *Miscanthus sinensis* in grass (Poaceae) family. Adults seen Jan–Oct.

■ HESPERIIDAE ■

Greenish Palm Dart ■ *Telicota bambusae* 竹长标弄蝶 WS 30–35mm

DESCRIPTION Small to medium skipper. Wings dark brown and orange. Can be difficult to distinguish from other *Telicota* skippers, with female sometimes indistinguishable in the field. Useful field marks for male include: on forewing upperside, orange streaks do reach termen (unlike in Dark and Hainan Palm Darts, pp. 46 and 47); on forewing upperside, male 'brand' centrally placed in dark brown streak (unlike in Pale Palm Dart, below). Brand wide and nearly fills streak. Greenish can also appear slightly darker than Pale. Sexes similar, though female does not have forewing brand. **DISTRIBUTION** Uncommonly identified in HK. Uncommon in HKI, NT and Lantau. Otherwise found from India to southern China, through mainland SE Asia, to Indonesia, Borneo, the Philippines and Australia. **HABITAT AND HABITS** Occurs in abandoned agricultural areas, gardens and secondary growth. Flight darting and fast. Active by day, with wings held half open at rest on flowers and grass. Often territorial, chasing others away before returning to rest. Adults sip nectar. Caterpillars feed on Hinds' Cane *Pseudosasa* (*Arundinaria*) *hindsii*, *Bambusa* bamboo and Elephant Grass *Pennisetum purpureum* in grass (Poaceae) family. Adults seen Jan–Nov. In HK, this species was previously referred to as *Telicota ancilla* 紅翅長標弄蝶.

Pale Palm Dart ■ *Telicota colon* 長標弄蝶 WS 35mm

DESCRIPTION Medium-sized skipper. Wings dark brown and orange. Can be difficult to distinguish from other *Telicota* skippers, with female sometimes indistinguishable in the field. Useful field marks for male include: on forewing upperside, orange streaks do reach termen (unlike in Dark and Hainan Palm Darts, pp. 46 and 47); on forewing upperside, male 'brand' off centre in brown streak (unlike in Greenish Palm Dart, above). Pale can also appear slightly lighter than Greenish. Sexes similar, though female does not have forewing brand. **DISTRIBUTION** Uncommonly identified in HK. Rare in HKI; uncommon in NT and Lantau. Otherwise found from India to southern China, through mainland SE Asia, western Indonesia and Australia. **HABITAT AND HABITS** Occurs in abandoned agricultural areas, gardens and secondary growth. Flight darting and fast. Active by day, with wings held half open at rest. Often territorial, chasing others away. Adults sip nectar. Caterpillars feed on grasses, e.g. Chinese Silvergrass *Miscanthus sinensis* and Elephant Grass *Pennisetum purpureum* in grass (Poaceae) family. Adults seen Jan–Oct.

HESPERIIDAE

Tamil Grass Dart ■ *Taractrocera ceramas* 草黃弄蝶 WS 30mm

DESCRIPTION Small skipper. Wings dark brown and orange. Hindwing-underside orange with dark brown marks. Antennae distinctly club shaped, unlike hooked antennae of many skippers. Sexes similar. **DISTRIBUTION** Rare. Not seen in HKI; rare in NT; uncommon in Lantau. Otherwise found locally from India to southern China, through mainland SE Asia. **HABITAT AND HABITS** Occurs in abandoned agricultural areas, gardens and secondary growth. Flight darting and fast. Active by day, with wings held half open at rest on flowers and grass. Often territorial, chasing others away before returning to rest. Adults sip nectar, especially from *Lantana* and *Vitex*. Caterpillars feed on Awned Panicgrass *Oplismenus compositus*, Cogon Grass *Imperata cylindrica*, Chinese Silvergrass *Miscanthus sinensis* and Broadleaf Carpetgrass *Axonopus compressus* in grass (Poaceae) family. Adults seen Mar–Apr.

Common Grass Dart ■ *Taractrocera maevius* 薇黃弄蝶 WS 20–30mm

DESCRIPTION Small skipper. Wings dark brown with cream stripes. Abdomen also striped dark brown and cream. Sexes similar. **DISTRIBUTION** Rare. Not seen in HKI; rare and local, only offshore on North and South Ninepin Islands, in NT; not seen in Lantau. Otherwise found from India to southern China, through mainland SE Asia. **HABITAT AND HABITS** Occurs in abandoned agricultural and other open, grassy areas in small local range. Flight low, flitting. Active by day, with wings held half open at rest. Adults sip nectar, and caterpillars feed on variety of grasses in grass (Poaceae) family, including Asian Rice *Oryza sativa*. Adults seen June–Aug.

■ Hesperiidae ■

Lesser Band Dart ■ *Potanthus trachala* 斷紋黃室弄蝶 WS 30–35mm

DESCRIPTION Small skipper. Wings dark brown and orange. Can be difficult to distinguish from the other three *Potanthus* skippers. Useful field marks include: on forewing upperside, orange marks in spaces M_2 and M_3 do not connect (as Indian Band Dart, below, and unlike the other two species); on hindwing upperside, space Rs lacks obvious spot, unlike in Indian, which has clear orange spot. Sexes similar. **DISTRIBUTION** Uncommonly identified in HK. Rare in HKI; uncommon in NT and Lantau. Otherwise found from southern China, through mainland SE Asia to western Indonesia. **HABITAT AND HABITS** Occurs in abandoned agricultural areas, gardens and secondary growth. Flight darting and fast. Active by day, with wings held half open at rest on flowers and grass. Often territorial, chasing others away before returning to rest. Adults sip nectar, especially from *Lantana* and *Vitex*. Caterpillars feed on grasses, including Pacific Island Silvergrass *Miscanthus floridulus*, Chinese Silvergrass *M. sinensis*, as well as *Ischaemum* grass and Tall Reed *Phragmites karka* in grass (Poaceae) family. Adults seen Feb–Oct.

Indian Band Dart ■ *Potanthus pseudomaesa* 擬黃室弄蝶 WS 30–35mm

DESCRIPTION Small skipper. Wings dark brown and orange. Can be difficult to distinguish from other *Potanthus* skippers. Useful field marks include: on forewing upperside, orange marks in spaces M_2 and M_3 do not connect (as in Indian Band Dart and unlike other two species); on hindwing upperside, space Rs shows an obvious spot (unlike in Lesser Band Dart, above, which lacks clear orange spot). Sexes similar. **DISTRIBUTION** Rarely identified in HK. Rare in HKI and NT; uncommon in Lantau. Otherwise found from India to southern China, through mainland SE Asia. **HABITAT AND HABITS** Occurs in abandoned agricultural areas, gardens and secondary growth. Flight darting and fast. Active by day, with wings held half open at rest on flowers and grass. Often territorial, chasing others away before returning to rest. Adults sip nectar, especially from *Lantana* and *Vitex*. Caterpillars feed on grasses, including Pacific Island Silvergrass *Miscanthus floridulus* and *Cymbopogon tortilis* in grass (Poaceae) family. Adults seen Mar–Dec.

= HESPERIIDAE =

Chinese Band Dart ■ *Potanthus confucius* 孔子黃室弄蝶 WS 25mm

DESCRIPTION Small skipper – smallest of *Potanthus* group in HK. Wings dark brown and orange. Can be difficult to distinguish from other *Potanthus* skippers. Useful field marks include: on forewing upperside, orange marks in spaces M_2 and M_3 connect (as in Yellow Band Dart, below, and unlike in other two species); on hindwing upperside, space Rs has no spot or only small spot, unlike in Yellow, which has large spot. Sexes similar. **DISTRIBUTION** Uncommonly identified in HK. Uncommon in HKI, NT and Lantau. Otherwise found from India to central and southern China, through mainland SE Asia. **HABITAT AND HABITS** Occurs in abandoned agricultural areas, gardens and secondary growth. Flight darting and fast. Active by day, with wings held half open at rest on flowers and grass. Often territorial, chasing others away before returning to rest. Adults sip nectar, especially from *Lantana* and *Vitex*. Caterpillars feed on Pacific Island Silvergrass *Miscanthus floridulus*, *Cymbopogon*, *Capillipedium*, *Eulalia*, *Ischaemum* and *Bambusa* plants in grass (Poaceae) family. Adults seen Feb–Nov.

Yellow Band Dart ■ *Potanthus pava* 寬紋黃室弄蝶 WS 25–30mm

DESCRIPTION Small skipper. Wings dark brown and orange. Can be difficult to distinguish from other *Potanthus* skippers. Useful field marks include: on forewing upperside, orange marks in spaces M_2 and M_3 connect, as in Chinese Band Dart (above), and unlike in other two species; on hindwing upperside, space Rs has large orange spot, unlike in Chinese, which has no spot or only small spot. Sexes similar. **DISTRIBUTION** Uncommonly identified in HK. Rare in HKI; fairly common in NT; uncommon in Lantau. Otherwise found from India to southern China, through mainland SE Asia. **HABITAT AND HABITS** Occurs in abandoned agricultural areas, gardens and secondary growth. Flight darting and fast. Active by day, with wings held half open at rest on flowers and grass. Often territorial, chasing others away before returning to rest. Adults sip nectar, especially from *Lantana* and *Vitex*. Caterpillars feed on *Bambusa* plants in grass (Poaceae) family. Adults seen Apr–Oct.

■ Hesperiidae ■

Common Straight Swift ■ *Parnara guttata* 直紋稻弄蝶 WS 35–40mm

DESCRIPTION Small to medium skipper. Wings dark brown, with several white forewing-spots and four light spots on hindwing-underside. When perched, hindwing-spots often form line alongside single white spot in centre of hindwing. Male also has two light spots in forewing radial cell. **DISTRIBUTION** Uncommon overall. Uncommon in HKI, NT and Lantau. Otherwise found from southern to northern China, Korea and Japan. **HABITAT AND HABITS** Occurs in abandoned agricultural areas and open grassland. Flight fast. Active by day; often territorial, with wings held vertically at rest. Adults sip nectar. Caterpillars feed on grasses including Chinese Silvergrass *Miscanthus sinensis*, Sasagrass *Lophatherum gracile*, Asian Rice *Oryza sativa*, *Microstegium ciliatum*, Scented Top *Capillipedium parviflorum* and Glutene-rice Grass *Apluda mutica* in grass (Poaceae) family. Adults seen Mar–Nov.

Continental Swift ■ *Parnara ganga* 曲紋稻弄蝶 WS 30–35mm

DESCRIPTION Small skipper, smaller than Common Straight Swift (above). Wings lighter brown, with several white forewing-spots and four light spots on hindwing-underside. When perched, hindwing-spots more disorganized and do not form line; often single white spot in hindwing-centre. Male does not have two light spots in forewing radial cell. **DISTRIBUTION** Uncommon overall. Uncommon in HKI Island, NT and Lantau. Otherwise found from India to southern China, through mainland SE Asia, to western Indonesia. **HABITAT AND HABITS** Occurs in abandoned agricultural areas and open grassland, especially wet areas. Flight fast. Active by day, and often territorial. Wings held vertically at rest. Adults sip nectar. Caterpillars feed on Native Rice Grass *Leersia hexandra* in grass (Poaceae) family. Adults seen May–Oct.

HESPERIIDAE

Oriental Straight Swift ■ *Parnara bada* 么紋稻弄蝶 WS 30–35mm

DESCRIPTION Small skipper, smaller than Common Straight Swift (opposite). Wings lighter brown, with few forewing white spots and no clear light spots on hindwing. When present, hindwing-spots tend to be poorly defined and small. Male does not have two light spots in forewing radial cell. **DISTRIBUTION** Rare overall. Rare in HKI, NT and Lantau. Otherwise found from India to southern China, through mainland SE Asia, to Indonesia, Borneo, the Philippines and Australia. **HABITAT AND HABITS** Occurs in abandoned agricultural areas and open grassland. Flight fast. Active by day, and often territorial. Wings held vertically at rest. Adults sip nectar. Caterpillars feed on Glutene-rice Grass *Apluda mutica* in grass (Poaceae) family. Adults seen Apr–Nov.

Formosan Swift ■ *Borbo cinnara* 秈弄蝶 WS 30–35mm

DESCRIPTION Small skipper, often with short antennae. Wings medium brown. Forewing radial cell plain with a few white spots, including one in cell CuA_2. Hindwing-underside can have 3–5 white spots, similar to Common Straight and Continental Swifts (opposite), though Formosan lacks white spot in hindwing-centre. **DISTRIBUTION** Common in HKI, NT and Lantau. Otherwise found from India to southern China, through mainland SE Asia, to Indonesia, Borneo and the Philippines. **HABITAT AND HABITS** Occurs in abandoned agricultural areas and open grassland, often at higher elevation. Flight fast. Active by day, with wings held half open at rest. Adults sip nectar. Caterpillars feed on Glutene-rice Grass *Apluda mutica*, Scented Top *Capillipedium parviflorum*, Goose Grass *Eleusine indica*, Guinea Grass *Panicum maximum*, *Digitaria*, *Microstegium ciliatum*, Hilograss *Paspalum conjugatum* and Palmgrass *Setaria palmifolia* in grass (Poaceae) family. Adults seen Apr–Dec.

◾ HESPERIIDAE ◾

Bevan's Swift ◾ *Pseudoborbo bevani* 擬稅弄蝶 WS 30mm

DESCRIPTION Small skipper. Wings medium brown, similar to those of Formosan Swift (p. 53) and *Parnara* swifts. Bevan's Swift smaller and paler, without clear white hindwing-spots. Forewing can have a few white spots, though they tend to be small and diffuse, and not in cell CuA_2. **DISTRIBUTION** Rare. Not seen in HKI; rare in NT; uncommon in Lantau. Otherwise found from India to southern China, through mainland SE Asia, to Borneo and the Philippines. **HABITAT AND HABITS** Occurs in abandoned agricultural areas, secondary growth and open grassland. Flight fast. Active by day, with wings held vertically or half open at rest. Adults sip nectar. Caterpillars feed on *Microstegium ciliatum* and *Ischaemum* plants in grass (Poaceae) family. Adults seen Mar–Oct.

■ HESPERIIDAE ■

Genus *Pelopidas*

The five HK species of *Pelopidas* skipper are often divided into two groups:
Branded *Pelopidas* Swifts Little Branded Swift *P. agna*, Small Branded Swift *P. mathias*, Large Branded Swift *P. subochracea*.
Non-branded *Pelopidas* Swifts Great Swift *P. assamensis*, Conjoined Swift *P. conjuncta*.

Little Branded Swift ■ *Pelopidas agna* 南亞穀弄蝶 WS 35mm

DESCRIPTION Small skipper. Wings medium brown with two white radial cell spots. Inside spot slightly ahead of outer spot, and a line drawn between the two would cross front of brand, unlike in Small Branded Swift (p. 56). Female very difficult to distinguish from Small, though a line drawn through the two spots points more anteriorly (v horizontally towards body in Small). Hindwing-underside has small white spots, usually smaller and less distinct than in Small. **DISTRIBUTION** Rarely identified in HK. Rare in HKI, NT and Lantau. Otherwise found from India to southern China, through mainland SE Asia, to Indonesia, Borneo, the Philippines and Australia. **HABITAT AND HABITS** Occurs in gardens and other open areas. Flight short and darting, often resting on flowers and grass. Active by day, with wings held half open at rest. Adults sip nectar. Caterpillars feed on Para Grass *Urochloa mutica*, Scented Top *Capillipedium parviflorum*, Hilograss *Paspalum conjugatum*, *Microstegium ciliatum* and *Ischaemum* plants in grass (Poaceae) family. Adults seen Mar–Nov.

▪ Hesperiidae ▪

Small Branded Swift ▪ *Pelopidas mathias* 隱紋穀弄蝶 WS 35mm

DESCRIPTION Small skipper. Wings medium brown with two white radial cell spots. Inside spot placed in line or slightly behind outer spot, and a line drawn between the two would cross centre of brand, unlike in Little Branded Swift (p. 55). Female very difficult to distinguish from Little, through a line drawn through the two spots points horizontally towards body (v more anteriorly in Little). Hindwing-underside has small white spots, usually slightly larger and more distinct than in Little. **DISTRIBUTION** Rarely identified in HK. Rare in HKI, NT and Lantau. Otherwise found from Sub-Saharan Africa, the Middle East and India, through China and Japan, to SE Asia. **HABITAT AND HABITS** Occurs in gardens and other open areas, often at high elevations. Flight short and darting, often resting on flowers and grass. Active by day, with wings held half open at rest. Adults sip nectar. Caterpillars feed on Scented Top *Capillipedium parviflorum*, *Cymbopogon tortilis*, Hilograss *Paspalum conjugatum*, *Microstegium ciliatum*, *Eulalia* and *Ischaemum* plants in grass (Poaceae) family. Adults seen year round.

▪ Hesperiidae ▪

Large Branded Swift ▪ *Pelopidas subochracea* 近赭穀弄蝶 WS 35mm

DESCRIPTION Small skipper, but can be a bit larger than Little and Small Branded Swifts (p. 55 and opposite). Wings orangish-brown with two white spots in radial cell. Male has clear white brand on forewing. Both sexes distinguished from Little and Small by orange tints as well as larger white spots on hindwing-underside. **DISTRIBUTION** Rarely identified in HK. Not seen in HKI; rare in NT and Lantau. Otherwise found from India to southern China, through mainland SE Asia. **HABITAT AND HABITS** Occurs in gardens and other open areas, often at high elevations. Flight short and darting, often resting on flowers and grass. Active by day, with wings held half open at rest. Adults sip nectar. Caterpillars feed on Nepalese Broom Grass *Thysanolaena latifolia* and Glutene-rice Grass *Apluda mutica* in grass (Poaceae) family. Adults seen Mar–Oct.

▪ HESPERIIDAE ▪

Great Swift ▪ *Pelopidas assamensis* 印度穀弄蝶 WS 50–55mm

DESCRIPTION Large skipper with dark brown wings. Male lacks brand. Distinguished by size and larger, brighter white spots than others in genus. **DISTRIBUTION** Uncommon in HKI, NT and Lantau. Otherwise found from India to southern China, through mainland SE Asia and western Indonesia. **HABITAT AND HABITS** Found singly in shady, wooded areas. Flight strong. Most active in the evening, with wings held half open at rest. Adults sip nectar. Caterpillars feed on Tiger Grass *Thysanolaena latifolia* (*maxima*) in grass (Poaceae) family. Adults seen Mar–Oct.

Conjoined Swift ▪ *Pelopidas conjuncta* 古銅穀弄蝶 WS 50mm

DESCRIPTION Large skipper with dark brown wings. Male lacks brand. Distinguished by size, yellower forewing-spots, and smaller, indistinct hindwing-spots than others in genus. **DISTRIBUTION** Uncommonly identified in HK. Rare in HKI; fairly common in NT; not seen in Lantau. Otherwise found from India to southern China, through mainland SE Asia, to Borneo and the Philippines. **HABITAT AND HABITS** Occurs in abandoned agricultural areas and open grassland. Flight fast. Active by day, often territorial and wings held half open at rest. Adults sip nectar. Caterpillars feed on Job's Tears *Coix lacryma-jobi*, *Microstegium ciliatum* and Chinese Silvergrass *Miscanthus sinensis* in grass (Poaceae) family. Adults seen Mar–Nov.

HESPERIIDAE

Contiguous Swift ■ *Polytremis lubricans* 黃紋孔弄蝶 WS 35–40mm

DESCRIPTION Small to medium skipper. Wings dark brown with auburn highlights. Yellow forewing- and hindwing-spots. Male lacks brand and sexes similar. **DISTRIBUTION** Uncommon in HKI and NT; fairly common in Lantau. Otherwise found from India to southern China, through mainland SE Asia, to Borneo and the Philippines. **HABITAT AND HABITS** Occurs in abandoned agricultural areas and open grassland. Flight fast. Active by day, often territorial, and wings held half open at rest. Adults sip nectar. Caterpillars feed on Pacific Island Silvergrass *Miscanthus floridulus* and Chinese Silvergrass *M. sinensis* in grass (Poaceae) family. Adults seen Mar–Nov.

Paintbrush Swift ■ *Baoris farri* 刺脛弄蝶 WS 40mm

DESCRIPTION Medium-sized skipper. Wings dark brown with variable amount of light forewing spotting, making identification difficult. Well-marked individuals have three white subapical spots. Hindwing plain, though male has dark brush of hair (usually only visible in the hand, see photo right), lacking in Colon and Dark Swifts (p. 60). Sexes otherwise similar. **DISTRIBUTION** Rarely identified in HK. Rare in HKI and NT; not seen in Lantau. Otherwise found from India to southern China, through mainland SE Asia and western Indonesia. **HABITAT AND HABITS** Occurs in secondary woodland. Flight fast. Active by day, often territorial and wings held half open at rest. Adults sip nectar. Caterpillars feed on *Bambusa* plants in grass (Poaceae) family. Adults seen Feb–Dec.

HESPERIIDAE

Colon Swift ■ *Caltoris bromus* 斑珂弄蝶 WS 40mm

DESCRIPTION Medium-sized skipper. Wings dark brown with variable light forewing spotting, making identification difficult. Well-marked individuals have three white subapical spots. Hindwing often plain, though underside can have 1–2 white spots, unlike in Dark Swift (below). Male lacks dark brush in Paintbrush Swift (p. 59). Sexes similar. **DISTRIBUTION** Uncommonly identified in HK. Not seen in HKI; uncommon in NT; rare in Lantau. Otherwise found from India to southern China, through mainland SE Asia. **HABITAT AND HABITS** Occurs in secondary woodland. Flight fast. Active by day, with wings held half open at rest. Adults seldom sip nectar. Caterpillars feed on Tall Reed *Phragmites karka* in grass (Poaceae) family. Adults seen Feb–Dec. Note that Dark Swift is sometimes called Colon Swift.

Dark Swift ■ *Caltoris cahira* 珂弄蝶 WS 40mm

DESCRIPTION Medium-sized skipper. Wings medium brown with variable amount of light spotting on forewing, making identification difficult. Well-marked individuals have two white subapical spots. Hindwing plain, lacking white spots seen on some Colon Swifts (above). Male lacks dark brush shown in Paintbrush Swift (p. 59). Sexes similar. **DISTRIBUTION** Uncommonly identified in HK. Rare in HKI and Lantau; uncommon in NT. Otherwise found from India to southern China, through mainland SE Asia. **HABITAT AND HABITS** Occurs in secondary woodland near bamboo. Flight fast. Active by day, with wings held half open at rest. Adults seldom sip nectar. Caterpillars feed on *Bambusa* plants in grass (Poaceae) family. Adults seen Mar–Oct. Alternative name: Colon Swift.

= PIERIDAE =

Three-spotted Grass Yellow ■ *Eurema blanda* 檗黃粉蝶 WS 45–50mm

DESCRIPTION Large grass yellow. Wings yellow with variable black markings above and brown markings below. Forewing radial cell usually marked with three black spots below, and hindwing-margin smoothly rounded. Sexes similar. DISTRIBUTION Common overall. Common in HKI and NT; fairly common in Lantau. Otherwise found from India and southern China, through mainland SE Asia, to Borneo, the Philippines and eastern Indonesia. HABITAT AND HABITS Occurs in parks and open areas near secondary woodland. Flight fast and close to the ground. Active by day. Adults sip nectar. Unusual in that it lays many eggs together, not just a single egg as in most butterflies. Caterpillars feed on a variety of plants in legume (Fabaceae) family, including Flamboyant *Delonix regia* and Lebbeck Tree *Albizia lebbeck*. Adults seen Feb–Nov.

Common Grass Yellow ■ *Eurema hecabe* 寬邊黃粉蝶 WS 45–50mm

DESCRIPTION The most common butterfly in HK; relatively large grass yellow. Wings yellow with variable black markings above and brown markings below. Forewing radial cell marked with 0–2 black spots, and hindwing-margin not smoothly rounded, appearing to 'bulge' slightly in middle (unlike in other two grass yellows illustrated). This feature can be subtle. Sexes similar. DISTRIBUTION Common in HKI, NT and Lantau. Otherwise found from India and southern China, through mainland SE Asia, to Borneo, the Philippines and eastern Indonesia. HABITAT AND HABITS Occurs widely in parks and open areas. Flight fast and close to the ground. Active by day. Adults sip nectar. Caterpillars feed on variety of plants in legume (Fabaceae) family, including *Albizia*, *Leucaena*, *Senna* and *Sesbania*. Others include Waxy Leaf *Breynia fruticosa* and Pop-gun Seed *Bridelia tomentosa* in spurge (Euphorbiaceae) family, Yellow Cow Wood *Cratoxylum cochinchinense* in St John's wort (Hypericaceae) family, and Hedge Sageretia *Sageretia thea* in buckthorn (Rhamnaceae) family. Adults seen year round.

▪ Pieridae ▪

Broad-bordered Grass Yellow ▪ *Eurema brigitta* 無標黃粉蝶
WS 35–45mm

DESCRIPTION Relatively small grass yellow. Wings yellow with black margins above. Diffuse brown markings below, though not in radial cell. Hindwing-margin smoothly rounded. Sexes similar. **DISTRIBUTION** Common in HKI Island, NT and Lantau. Otherwise found from India and southern China, through mainland SE Asia, to Borneo, the Philippines and eastern Indonesia. **HABITAT AND HABITS** Occurs in grassy and abandoned agricultural areas at low elevation. Flight slow and erratic, close to the ground. Active by day. Adults sip nectar. Caterpillars feed on Fishbone Cassia *Chamaecrista mimosoides* in legume (Fabaceae) family. Adults seen Feb–Dec, especially Sep.

Spotless Grass Yellow ▪ *Eurema laeta* 尖角黃粉蝶 (not illustrated)

Very rarely reported in HK in northern NT. Generally similar to other *Eurema* grass yellows in HK and distinguished by distinctively pointed forewing with black corners. Also, outer hindwing corners not rounded and appear cut at an angle, similar to Common Grass Yellow (p. 61).

Tailed Sulphur ▪ *Dercas verhuelli* 檀方粉蝶 WS 60–70mm

DESCRIPTION Large sulphur butterfly with distinctive shape. Wings yellow and angled in unique way, with brown markings above and below. Sexes similar. **DISTRIBUTION** Uncommon. Not seen in HKI and Lantau; fairly common in NT. Otherwise found from India and southern China, through mainland SE Asia, to Borneo. **HABITAT AND HABITS** Occurs in forest, where it flies slowly and erratically in shady undergrowth. Active by day, often resting on undersides of leaves. Adults occasionally sip nectar. Caterpillars feed on Bentham's Rosewood *Dalbergia benthamii* in legume (Fabaceae) family. Adults seen Feb–Nov, especially Mar.

PIERIDAE

Lemon Emigrant *Catopsilia pomona* 遷粉蝶 WS 60mm

DESCRIPTION Large sulphur butterfly. Male white above, with yellow at base. Female yellow, with black margins above and variety of brown spots below. Several forms, which can differ in amount of brown present in female. **DISTRIBUTION** Common in HKI, NT and Lantau. Otherwise found from India and southern China, through mainland SE Asia, Indonesia, Borneo, the Philippines, and Australia to Fiji. **HABITAT AND HABITS** Occurs in parks and open shrubland, where it flies strongly. Occasionally seen puddling or migrating in large groups. Active by day. Adults sip nectar. Caterpillars feed on Burmese Rosewood *Pterocarpus indicus*, Kassod Tree *Senna* (*Cassia*) *siamea* and Golden Shower Tree *Cassia fistula* in legume (Fabaceae) family. Adults seen year round, especially July–Sep.

Female

Male

Female

■ PIERIDAE ■

Mottled Emigrant ■ *Catopsilia pyranthe* 梨花遷粉蝶 WS 60mm

DESCRIPTION Large sulphur butterfly. Adults white above with black forewing-tips. Yellow below, with female having brown markings. Both sexes have faint striations below, a key difference from Lemon Emigrant (p. 63). **DISTRIBUTION** Common in HKI, NT and Lantau. Otherwise found from India and southern China, through mainland SE Asia, Indonesia, Borneo, the Philippines, and Australia to Fiji. **HABITAT AND HABITS** Occurs in parks and open shrubland, where it flies strongly. Occasionally seen puddling or migrating in large groups. Active by day. Adults sip nectar. Caterpillars feed on Coffee Senna *Senna occidentalis* in legume (Fabaceae) family. Adults seen year round.

Male   *Female*

Great Orange Tip ■ *Hebomoia glaucippe* 鶴頂粉蝶 WS 80–90mm

DESCRIPTION Large pierid butterfly. Adults white above with orange and black forewing-tips. Female has black hindwing-margin above. Both sexes have mottled dead-leaf pattern below, to reduce detection by predators. **DISTRIBUTION** Uncommon. Fairly common in HKI; uncommon in NT and Lantau. Otherwise found from India and southern China, through mainland SE Asia, Indonesia, Borneo and the Philippines. **HABITAT AND HABITS** Found widely in HK, from urban parks to forested hillsides. Active by day, with fast, erratic and high flight. Males occasionally descend to mudpuddle, and adults sip nectar. Caterpillars feed on Canton Caper *Capparis cantoniensis* and Spider Tree *Crateva unilocularis* (*religiosa*) in caper (Capparaceae) family. Adults seen nearly year round, especially May–June.

▪ PIERIDAE ▪

Yellow Orange Tip ▪ *Ixias pyrene* 橙粉蝶 WS 50–60mm

DESCRIPTION Medium to large pierid butterfly. Adults yellowish above with black wing-tips and orange band in male. Yellow below, with brown markings in dry-season form.
DISTRIBUTION Uncommon in HKI, NT and Lantau. Otherwise found from India and southern China, through mainland SE Asia, to Borneo. **HABITAT AND HABITS** Most often seen in wooded areas near host plant, at a range of elevations. Active by day. Males mudpuddle, and adults sip nectar. Caterpillars feed on Canton Caper *Capparis cantoniensis* in caper (Capparaceae) family. Adults seen nearly year round, especially Oct.

Male

Male

Female

Female

= PIERIDAE =

Indian Cabbage White ■ *Pieris canidia* 東方菜粉蝶 WS 50–55mm

Female

DESCRIPTION Medium-sized pierid butterfly. Male white above with black wing-tips and several black spots, including on hindwing-margin. Pale yellow below. Female pale yellow throughout, with similar black wing-tips and spotting. **DISTRIBUTION** Common in HKI, NT and Lantau. Otherwise found from India to China and Korea, through mainland SE Asia. **HABITAT AND HABITS** Seen widely, especially near vegetable gardens and agricultural areas. Active by day, even during cloudy periods, roosting in large congregations before sunset. Flight slow, and adults sip nectar. Caterpillars feed on several plants in mustard (Brassicales) order, including Garden Nasturtium *Tropaeolum majus* in nasturtium (Tropaeolaceae) family, *Cleome* in spider flower (Cleomaceae) family, and especially different varieties of *Brassica*, *Rorippa* and *Nasturtium* cabbages and mustards in mustard (Brassicaceae) family. Main native host plants include Diverse-leaf Yellowcress *Rorippa indica*, *R. dubia* and Watercress *Nasturtium officinale*. Adults seen year round.

Male

Male

▪ Pieridae ▪

Small Cabbage White ▪ *Pieris rapae* 菜粉蝶 WS 50–55mm

DESCRIPTION Medium-sized pierid butterfly, less common than Indian Cabbage White (opposite). Male white above with black wing-tips and 2–3 black spots, and pale yellow below. Less black on wing-tips than in Indian, and Small lacks black spots on hindwing. Female white above (v yellow in Indian), and pale yellow with black wing-tips below, like male. DISTRIBUTION Fairly common in HKI, NT and Lantau. Otherwise Palearctic in distribution, from Europe to the Middle East, Central Asia, to China, Korea and Japan. Introduced to North America, Australia, New Zealand and other locations. HABITAT AND HABITS Seen widely, especially near vegetable gardens and agricultural areas. Migratory at times, and active by day. Flight slow, and adults sip nectar. Caterpillars feed on several introduced plants in mustard (Brassicales) order, including *Cleome* plants in spider flower (Cleomaceae) family and different varieties of *Brassica oleracea* vegetable in mustard (Brassicaceae) family. Adults seen year round, especially Apr. One of the few HK butterflies that is probably not (entirely) native, having spread by introduction of its host plants for agriculture and landscaping.

Common Albatross ▪ *Appias albina* 白翅尖粉蝶 WS 60mm

DESCRIPTION Medium-sized pierid butterfly. Male bright white above and yellowish below, with pointed forewing. Female white above with black margins. Forewing has black margins below, lacking in hindwing. DISTRIBUTION Rare in HKI, NT and Lantau. Otherwise found from India to southern China, through mainland SE Asia, to Borneo and the Philippines. HABITAT AND HABITS Seen in forests and open secondary growth. Flight rapid, and adults sip nectar. Caterpillars feed on *Capparis* plants in caper (Capparaceae) family and *Drypetes* plants in iron plum (Putranjivaceae) family. Adults only seen in narrow timeframe, from late Apr through mid-May.

Male

Female

67

▪ Pieridae ▪

Common Gull ▪ *Cepora nerissa* 黑脈園粉蝶 WS 50–60mm

DESCRIPTION Medium-sized pierid butterfly. White above with black forewing-tips. Yellowish below. Wet-season form has distinctive dark grey vein markings. Sexes similar. **DISTRIBUTION** Fairly common in HKI, NT and Lantau. Otherwise found from India and southern China, through mainland SE Asia, to western Indonesia, Borneo and the Philippines. **HABITAT AND HABITS** Seen in open areas and secondary woodland. Active by day, when it may be seen at hilltops. Flight strong. Males mudpuddle, and adults sip nectar, especially from *Lantana*. Caterpillars feed on Canton Caper *Capparis cantoniensis* in caper (Capparaceae) family. Adults seen nearly year round, especially May and June.

Wet-season form

Dry-season form

Dry-season form

PIERIDAE

Lesser Gull ▪ *Cepora nadina* 青園粉蝶 WS 60mm

DESCRIPTION Medium-sized pierid butterfly. Male white above with broad black margins. Yellow underneath with charcoal veins and 1–2 white areas. Female charcoal above with white patches in centre of forewing. **DISTRIBUTION** Not previously known in HK, but uncommon since 2021. Rare in HKI; uncommon in NT and Lantau. Otherwise found from India and southern China, through mainland SE Asia, to western Indonesia. **HABITAT AND HABITS** Occurs in forest and woodland, in more closed situations than Common Gull (opposite). Adults active by day, flying rapidly along paths and streams, sipping nectar. Males visit damp soil or sand. Caterpillars feed on *Capparis* plants in caper (Capparaceae) family. Adults seen Apr–Dec.

Male

Male

Female

■ Pieridae ■

Spotted Sawtooth ■ *Prioneris thestylis* 鋸粉蝶 WS 65–75mm

DESCRIPTION Large pierid butterfly. Distinctive yellow and black pattern below, similar to jezebels but with darker yellow and no red. Male forewing white with black edges; female with more yellow. Male also has microscopic 'teeth' on leading edge of forewing, hence the name 'sawtooth'. **DISTRIBUTION** Uncommon. Rare in HKI; uncommon in NT and Lantau. Otherwise found from India and southern China, through mainland SE Asia. **HABITAT AND HABITS** Occurs near forest. Active by day, when males often hilltop and puddle. Flight very fast, and wings held vertically at rest. Adults sip nectar. Caterpillars feed on *Capparis* and *Crateva* plants in caper (Capparaceae) family. Adults typically seen Mar–July.

Red-based Jezebel ■ *Delias pasithoe* 報喜斑粉蝶 WS 70mm

DESCRIPTION Large pierid butterfly. At rest, characteristic red base to yellow hindwing. Veins black. Black and white above, with no red patch. Female has darker brown smudges; otherwise sexes similar. **DISTRIBUTION** Common in HKI, NT and Lantau. Otherwise found from India and southern China, through mainland SE Asia, to western Indonesia, Borneo and the Philippines. **HABITAT AND HABITS** Occurs near forest. Active by day. Flight slow, and wings held vertically at rest. Aposematic yellow and especially red colouring a warning to predators that it is toxic (in this regard, jezebel butterflies are mimicked by several day-flying moths). Males often hilltop, and adults sip nectar, especially from *Ligustrum*, *Syzygium* and *Bischofia*. Unusual in that many eggs are laid together, not just a single egg as in most butterflies. Caterpillars feed on Cinnamon Mistletoe *Scurrula parasitica* and Common Chinese Mistletoe *Macrosolon cochinchinensis* in showy mistletoe (Loranthaceae) family and *Dendrotrophe varians* (*frutescens*) in sandalwood (Santalaceae) family, both in Santalales order of mistletoes and sandalwoods. Notably, both of these plant families are considered parasitic, taking nutrients from other plants. Adults seen year round, though migrants swell HK population in winter and spring.

■ Pieridae ■

Red-breast Jezebel ■ *Delias acalis* 紅腋斑粉蝶 WS 65–75mm

DESCRIPTION Large pierid butterfly. From above, distinguished from Red-based and Painted Jezebels (opposite and below) by red patch at wing-base. Hindwing mainly white (light yellow in male) below with broad red base and small orange patch. Sexes similar. **DISTRIBUTION** Rare in HKI and NT; not seen in Lantau. Otherwise found from India and southern China, through mainland SE Asia. **HABITAT AND HABITS** Occurs near forest. Active by day. Flight slow, and wings held vertically at rest. Males seen hilltopping and puddling. Adults sip nectar. Caterpillars feed on Malayan Mistletoe *Dendrophthoe pentandra* and Common Chinese Mistletoe *Macrosolen cochinchinensis* in showy mistletoe (Loranthaceae) family. Adults typically seen Mar–July.

Painted Jezebel ■ *Delias hyparete* 優越斑粉蝶 WS 60–70mm

DESCRIPTION Medium to large pierid butterfly. White above with black veins. At rest, yellow hindwing with red submarginal spots near trailing edge. Sexes similar. **DISTRIBUTION** Uncommon. Not seen in HKI and Lantau; fairly common in NT. Otherwise found from India and southern China, through mainland SE Asia, to western Indonesia, Borneo and the Philippines. **HABITAT AND HABITS** Occurs near forest. Active by day, when males often hilltop and puddle. Flight slow, and wings held vertically at rest. Adults sip nectar, especially from *Albizia*. Unusual in that many eggs laid together, not just single egg as in most butterflies. Caterpillars feed on Common Chinese Mistletoe *Macrosolen cochinchinensis* in showy mistletoe (Loranthaceae) family. Adults seen year round.

NYMPHALIDAE

Common Tiger Butterfly ■ *Danaus genutia* 虎斑蝶 WS 80mm

DESCRIPTION Large danaid tiger butterfly. Wings orange with black veins. Diagonal white patch near forewing-tip. Male has black patch in centre of hindwing, otherwise sexes similar. **DISTRIBUTION** Common in HKI, NT and Lantau. Otherwise found from India and southern China, through mainland SE Asia, to western Indonesia, Borneo and the Philippines. **HABITAT AND HABITS** Occurs in a wide variety of open habitats. Active by day. Flight slow. Adults fan wings slowly while sipping nectar. Migratory, and in late autumn through Dec, adults may be found in large groups with other danaid butterflies, hanging motionless or gliding between Rattleweed *Crotalaria retusa* or other plants. Caterpillars feed on *Graphistemma* (*Cynanchum*) *pictum* (*graphistemmatoides*) in milkweed (Asclepiadoideae) subfamily of dogbane (Apocynaceae) family. Adults seen year round, especially Aug–Nov.

Plain Tiger Butterfly ■ *Danaus chrysippus* 金斑蝶 WS 70mm

DESCRIPTION Large danaid tiger butterfly. Wings orange, without black veins. Wing-tips black, and diagonal white patch near forewing-tips. Sexes similar. **DISTRIBUTION** Fairly common in HKI, NT and Lantau. Otherwise found from the Mediterranean through the Middle East, Africa, India, southern China and southern Japan, through mainland SE Asia, to Indonesia, Borneo and the Philippines. **HABITAT AND HABITS** Occurs in a wide variety of open habitats. Active by day. Flight slow and near the ground. Adults fan wings slowly while sipping nectar. Unlike related danaids, not found in large groups in autumn and early winter. Caterpillars feed on Tropical Milkweed *Asclepias curassavica* in milkweed (Asclepiadoideae) subfamily of dogbane (Apocynaceae) family. Adults seen year round, especially June–Nov.

NYMPHALIDAE

Ceylon Blue Glassy Tiger Butterfly ■ *Ideopsis similis* 擬旖斑蝶
WS 85mm

DESCRIPTION Large danaid tiger butterfly. Black with bluish-white spots and stripes. Similar to a few related danaid butterflies, as well as mimics Common Mime Swallowtail and Red Ring Skirt (pp. 20 and 114), but a close look reveals consistent differences in pattern of light spots. For instance, light spots larger in this species than in Blue or Dark Blue Tiger Butterflies (pp. 74 and 75), and generally more organized than in Blue. Also reddish-purple tone below. Sexes similar. **DISTRIBUTION** Common in HKI, NT and Lantau. Otherwise found from India, southern China and Japan, through mainland SE Asia. **HABITAT AND HABITS** Occurs in wide variety of open habitats. Active by day. Flight slow and near the ground. Adults fan wings slowly while sipping nectar, especially from Billygoat Weed *Ageratum conyzoides*. In late autumn through Dec, adults may be found in large groups with other danaid butterflies, hanging motionless or gliding between Rattleweed *Crotalaria retusa* or other plants. Caterpillars feed on *Vincetoxicum hirsutum* (formerly *Tylophora ovata*) in milkweed (Asclepiadoideae) subfamily of dogbane (Apocynaceae) family. Adults seen year round.

NYMPHALIDAE

Blue Tiger Butterfly ■ *Tirumala limniace* 青斑蝶 WS 90mm

DESCRIPTION
Large danaid tiger butterfly. Black with bluish-white spots and stripes; overall darker than Ceylon Blue Glassy Tiger Butterfly and lighter than Dark Blue Tiger Butterfly (pp. 73 and opposite). Similar to mimics Common Mime Swallowtail and Red Ring Skirt (pp. 20 and 114), but close look reveals consistent differences in pattern of light spots. Also brown tone below. Sexes similar.
DISTRIBUTION
Common in HKI and NT; fairly common in Lantau. Otherwise found from India and southern China, through mainland SE Asia, to Indonesia, Borneo and the Philippines. **HABITAT AND HABITS** Occurs in wooded areas. Active by day. Flight fairly slow but can be at treetop level. Adults fan wings slowly while sipping nectar, especially from Billygoat Weed *Ageratum conyzoides*. In late autumn through Dec, adults may be found in large groups with other danaid butterflies, hanging motionless or gliding between Rattleweed *Crotalaria retusa* or other plants. Caterpillars in HK known to feed on Jukti *Wattaka* (*Dregea*) *volubilis* in milkweed (Asclepiadoideae) subfamily of dogbane (Apocynaceae) family. Adults seen year round, especially Aug–Jan.

▪ NYMPHALIDAE ▪

Dark Blue Tiger Butterfly ▪ *Tirumala septentrionis* 嗇青斑蝶 WS 90mm

DESCRIPTION Large danaid tiger butterfly. Black with bluish-white spots and stripes; overall darker than Ceylon Blue and Blue Tiger Butterflies (pp. 73 and opposite). Sexes similar. **DISTRIBUTION** Rare in HKI, NT and Lantau. Otherwise found from India and southern China, through mainland SE Asia, to Indonesia, Borneo and the Philippines. **HABITAT AND HABITS** Found in wooded areas. Active by day. Flight fairly slow but can be at treetop level. Adults fan wings slowly while sipping nectar, especially from Billygoat Weed *Ageratum conyzoides*. Caterpillars feed on Tropical Milkweed *Asclepias curassavica* in milkweed (Asclepiadoideae) subfamily of dogbane (Apocynaceae) family. Adults seen year round.

Glassy Tiger Butterfly ▪ *Parantica aglea* 絹斑蝶 WS 75–80mm

DESCRIPTION Large danaid tiger butterfly. Dark brown, including margins and veins. Dark areas interspersed with extensive white markings, making it the lightest of this group. Sexes similar. **DISTRIBUTION** Common in HKI and NT; fairly common in Lantau. Otherwise found from India and southern China, through mainland SE Asia, to western Indonesia and the Philippines. **HABITAT AND HABITS** Occurs in secondary growth and open wooded areas at lower elevation. Active by day. Flight slow and gliding. Adults fan wings slowly while sipping nectar, especially from Billygoat Weed *Ageratum conyzoides*. In late autumn through Dec, adults may be found in large groups with other danaid butterflies, hanging motionless or gliding between Rattleweed *Crotalaria retusa* or other plants. Caterpillars feed on *Vincetoxicum hirsutum* (formerly *Tylophora ovata*) in milkweed (Asclepiadoideae) subfamily of dogbane (Apocynaceae) family. Adults seen year round.

NYMPHALIDAE

Chestnut Tiger Butterfly ■ *Parantica sita* 大絹斑蝶 WS 90–100mm

DESCRIPTION Large danaid tiger butterfly, the largest in HK. Dark reddish-brown, including margins and veins. Dark areas interspersed with large white patches. Unlike Chocolate Tiger Butterfly (below), abdomen dark. Sexes similar. **DISTRIBUTION** Rare in HKI, NT and Lantau. Otherwise found from India to central and southern China and Japan, through mainland SE Asia. Northern populations migrate south in autumn and winter. **HABITAT AND HABITS** Occurs in woodland from lowlands to hillsides. Active by day. Flight fairly strong, often sailing at treetop level. Adults sip nectar, especially from Billygoat Weed *Ageratum conyzoides* and *Citrus* blossoms. Caterpillars feed on *Vincetoxicum hirsutum* (formerly *Tylophora ovata*) and Wax Plant *Hoya carnosa* in milkweed (Asclepiadoideae) subfamily of dogbane (Apocynaceae) family. Adults typically seen Jan–June, rarely in late autumn.

Chocolate Tiger Butterfly ■ *Parantica melaneus* 黑絹斑蝶 WS 90mm

DESCRIPTION Large danaid tiger butterfly. Dark reddish-brown, including margins and veins. Dark areas interspersed with large white patches. Similar to Chestnut Tiger Butterfly (above), but with additional blue line below on hindwing, and orange abdomen. Sexes similar. **DISTRIBUTION** Rare in HKI and NT; not seen in Lantau. Otherwise found from India to southern China, through mainland SE Asia. **HABITAT AND HABITS** Occurs in woodland. Active by day. Flight fairly strong, often sailing at treetop level. Adults sip nectar, especially from Billygoat Weed *Ageratum conyzoides* and *Citrus* blossoms. Caterpillars feed on *Jasminanthes mucronata* and *Marsdenia tinctoria* in milkweed (Asclepiadoideae) subfamily of dogbane (Apocynaceae) family. Adults seen Nov–Jan.

NYMPHALIDAE

Common Crow Butterfly ■ *Euploea core* 幻紫斑蝶 WS 85mm

DESCRIPTION Large danaid crow butterfly. From above, dark brown without clear purplish-blue on forewing. This is diagnostic. From below, male is plainest of this genus and only species lacking white marginal spotting. Female identified by lack of white marginal spotting (in plain individuals) or when marginal spots are present, they are shorter and more rounded than in other species. More variable than other crow butterflies. **DISTRIBUTION** Fairly common in HKI, NT and Lantau. Otherwise found from India to southern China, through mainland SE Asia, to Borneo, the Philippines and Australia. **HABITAT AND HABITS** Occurs in gardens and wooded areas. Active by day. Flight gliding at low or moderate height, with wings fixed in shallow 'V'. Adults sip nectar. Migratory species that increases in autumn, when communal roosts are common. These generally precede the large Dec gatherings with other danaid butterflies, when they hanging motionless or glide between Rattleweed *Crotalaria retusa* or other plants. Caterpillars feed on *Toxocarpus wightianus* and Oleander *Nerium oleander* in dogbane (Apocynaceae) family. Adults seen year round, especially July–Jan.

More spotted female form

Typical male/female

NYMPHALIDAE

Blue-spotted Crow Butterfly ■ *Euploea midamus* 藍點紫斑蝶
WS 85–95mm

Female

DESCRIPTION Large danaid crow butterfly. Dark brown with dark purplish-blue on forewing and marginal white hindwing-spots. Male distinguished by combination of blue forewing upperside patch that does not reach margin. Common Crow Butterfly (p. 77) does not have blue here, and Striped Blue Crow Butterfly (opposite) has more blue that extends to margin. Also by row of submarginal light hindwing-spots below. Female identified by blue upperside-forewing patch. Common does not have blue here. Also by row of submarginal light hindwing-spots. Striped has long white lines, rather than spots. This and other *Euploea* crow butterflies similar to mimics Common Mime Swallowtail (p. 20), and Danaid and Great Eggflies (pp. 121 and 122), but close look reveals consistent differences. **DISTRIBUTION** Common in HKI, NT and Lantau. Otherwise found from India to southern China, through mainland SE Asia, to Borneo and the Philippines. **HABITAT AND HABITS** Occurs in wooded areas and nearby open spaces. Active by day. Flight gliding at low or moderate height, with wings fixed in shallow 'V'. Adults sip nectar, especially from Billygoat Weed *Ageratum conyzoides* and Prickly Ash *Zanthoxylum avicennae*. Migratory species that increases in autumn, when communal roosts are common. These generally precede the large Dec gatherings with other danaid butterflies, when they hanging motionless or glide between Rattleweed *Crotalaria retusa* or other plants. Caterpillars feed on Goat Horns *Strophanthus divaricatus* in dogbane (Apocynoideae) subfamily of dogbane (Apocynaceae) family. Adults seen year round, especially July–Jan.

Male

NYMPHALIDAE

Striped Blue Crow Butterfly ▪ *Euploea mulciber* 異型紫斑蝶 WS 90mm

DESCRIPTION Large danaid crow butterfly. Dark brown with dark purplish-blue on forewing and white hindwing markings. Male distinguished by combination of blue forewing-upperside patch that reaches margin (Common Crow Butterfly, p. 77, does not have blue here, and Blue-spotted Crow Butterfly, opposite, has less blue that does not extend to the margin), and minimal submarginal light hindwing-spots below. Female has blue forewing-upperside patch and diagnostic long white stripes below on hindwing. **DISTRIBUTION** Uncommon in HKI, NT and Lantau. Otherwise found from India to southern China, through mainland SE Asia, to Borneo and the Philippines. **HABITAT AND HABITS** Occurs in wooded areas. Active by day. Flight gliding at low or moderate height, with wings fixed in shallow 'V'. Adults sip nectar, especially from Billygoat Weed *Ageratum conyzoides* and Prickly Ash *Zanthoxylum avicennae*. Caterpillars feed on *Toxocarpus wightianus* in dogbane (Apocynaceae) family. Adults seen June–Nov.

Male

Female

NYMPHALIDAE

Tawny Rajah ■ *Charaxes bernardus* 白帶螯蛺蝶 WS 65–80mm

Male form sinensis

DESCRIPTION Medium to large butterfly. Male orange above with black wing-tips. Three forms with different colours across middle of forewing – orange (*sinensis*), tawny, and white (*bernardus*). Underneath mainly brown with light violet gloss. Female similar, but larger and with short tail on hindwing. **DISTRIBUTION** Fairly common in HKI, NT and Lantau. Otherwise found from India to central and southern China, through mainland SE Asia, to Borneo. **HABITAT AND HABITS** Occurs in wooded areas, where male can be territorial from an elevated perch. Active by day, with very strong flight. Wings closed at rest. Adults feed on citrus sap, overripe fruits and animal faeces. Caterpillars feed on Acronychia *Acronychia pedunculata* in citrus (Rutaceae) family, plus Bolly Beech *Litsea glutinosa* and Camphor Tree *Cinnamomum camphora* in laurel (Lauraceae) family. Adults seen year round.

Female

Male form bernardus

■ NYMPHALIDAE ■

Yellow Rajah ■ *Charaxes marmax* 螯蛱蝶 WS 80mm

DESCRIPTION Medium to large butterfly. Similar to Tawny Rajah (opposite), but wing-tips less black above, and below yellow more evenly coloured. Sexes similar, though female larger than male. **DISTRIBUTION** Rare overall. Not seen in HKI and Lantau; uncommon in NT. Otherwise found from India to southern China, through mainland SE Asia. **HABITAT AND HABITS** Male occurs in uplands, and female in wooded areas. Male can be territorial from an elevated perch. Active by day, with very strong flight. Wings closed at rest. Adults feed on citrus sap, overripe fruits and animal faeces. Caterpillars feed on Purging Croton *Croton tiglium* in spurge (Euphorbiaceae) family. Adults seen Mar–Dec.

Common Nawab ■ *Polyura athamas* 窄斑凤尾蛱蝶 WS 60–70mm

DESCRIPTION Medium-sized butterfly. Dark brown with broad cream band (slightly greenish) above and below. Two short wing-tails. Sexes similar, though female larger than male. **DISTRIBUTION** Uncommon in HKI, NT and Lantau. Otherwise found from India to southern China, through mainland SE Asia, to Borneo and the Philippines. **HABITAT AND HABITS** Occurs in forested areas. Active by day, with strong flight at canopy level. Males hilltop and can be very territorial from an elevated perch. Wings closed at rest. Adults feed on citrus sap, overripe fruits and animal faeces. Caterpillars feed on Monkey-Pod *Archidendron clypearia*, Soap-pod Tree *Senegelia* (*Acacia*) *rugata* (*concinna*, *sinuata*), Lebbeck Tree *Albizia lebbeck*, *A. corniculata*, White Leadtree *Leucaena leucocephala* and Yellow Flame Tree *Peltophorum pterocarpum* in legume (Fabaceae) family. Adults seen year round.

81

▪ Nymphalidae ▪

Shan Nawab ▪ *Polyura nepenthes* 忘憂尾蛺蝶 WS 70mm (male), 90mm (female)

DESCRIPTION Medium to large butterfly. Creamy white above with black wing-tips, lacking broad black hindwing-margin of Great Nawab (below). Creamy white below without 'cross-bar' (nearly) connecting two orange forewing-bands as in Great. Two short wing-tails. Sexes similar, though female larger than male. **DISTRIBUTION** Uncommon in HKI and NT; rare in Lantau. Otherwise found from central and southern China, through mainland SE Asia. **HABITAT AND HABITS** Occurs in forested areas. Active by day, with strong flight at canopy level. Males hilltop and can be very territorial from an elevated perch. Wings closed at rest. Adults feed on citrus sap, overripe fruits and animal faeces. Caterpillars feed on *Archidendron lucidum* in legume (Fabaceae) family and Smooth-fruited Ventilago *Ventilago leiocarpa* in buckthorn (Rhamnaceae) family. Adults seen Apr through Nov.

Great Nawab ▪ *Polyura eudamippus* 大二尾蛺蝶 WS 100mm (male), 120mm (female)

DESCRIPTION Large butterfly. Creamy white above with black wing-tips and broad black hindwing-margin, lacking in Shan Nawab (above). Creamy white below with distinctive 'cross-bar' that (nearly) connects two orange forewing-bands, also lacking in Shan. Two short wing-tails. Sexes similar, though female larger than male. **DISTRIBUTION** Only consistently seen in HK since 2021. Now rare but regular. Not seen in HKI and Lantau; rare in NT. Otherwise found from India to southern China, through mainland SE Asia. **HABITAT AND HABITS** Occurs in forested areas. Active by day, with strong flight at canopy level. Males hilltop and can be very territorial from an elevated perch. Wings closed at rest. Adults feed on citrus sap, overripe fruits and animal faeces. Caterpillars feed on *Archidendron lucidum* in legume (Fabaceae) family. Adults seen Apr through Sep.

NYMPHALIDAE

Common Palmfly
Elymnias hypermnestra 翠袖鋸眼蝶 WS 65–70mm

DESCRIPTION Medium-sized butterfly with serrated wing-margins. Dark brown with grey triangle near forewing apex below. Forewing purplish above with lighter markings near margin. One distinctive white spot near hindwing costa, larger in female than male and visible at rest. **DISTRIBUTION** Probably introduced to HK through ornamental palm trade in around 1983. Now common in HKI and NT; fairly common in Lantau. Otherwise found from India and southern China, through mainland SE Asia. **HABITAT AND HABITS** Occurs in parks and wooded areas. Active by day, with female flying and male often defending a territory from a perch within 1–2 metres of the ground. Male chases intruders and attempts to mate with passing females. Courting pairs engage in swirling 'dance', rapidly circling each other a few metres above the ground. Wings closed at rest. Adults feed on overripe fruits. Caterpillars feed on variety of ornamental palms in palm (Arecaceae) family, including Pygmy Date Palm *Phoenix roebelenii*, Areca Palm *Dypsis* (*Chrysalidocarpus*) *lutescens* and Alexandra Palm *Archontophoenix alexandrae*. Adults seen year round. One of the few HK butterflies that is probably not (entirely) native, having spread by introduction of host plants for landscaping.

Large Faun
Faunis eumeus 串珠環蝶 WS 70mm

DESCRIPTION Distinctive medium-sized butterfly. Orangish-brown above and below, with female having clearer orange forewing-band than male. Row of cream dots below. **DISTRIBUTION** Common in HKI, NT and Lantau. Otherwise found from India and southern China, through mainland SE Asia. **HABITAT AND HABITS** Occurs in wooded areas. Active by day, with slow and meandering flight. Wings closed at rest. Adults feed on overripe fruits. Unusual in that many eggs are laid together, not just a single egg as in most butterflies. Caterpillars feed on a variety of monocotyledonous plants, including Spiny Date Palm *Phoenix loureiroi* (*hanceana*) in palm (Arecaceae) family, Chinese Greenbrier *Smilax china* and Opaque Greenbrier *S. lanceifolia* in greenbrier (Smilaceae) family, *Pandanus* species in screwpine (Pandanaceae) family and Lily Turf *Liriope spicata* in asparagus (Asparagaceae) family. Adults seen year round.

Male

◾ NYMPHALIDAE ◾

Common Duffer ◾ *Discophora sondaica* 鳳眼方環蝶 WS 70–80mm

DESCRIPTION Medium-sized butterfly with 'pointed' look due to sharply angled apex. Brown above and below with inner half of wings darker than outer half. Hindwings have two subtle eye-spots below. Female paler than male, with larger white spots above. **DISTRIBUTION** Uncommon. Fairly common in HKI and NT; rare in Lantau. Otherwise found from India and southern China, through mainland SE Asia, to Borneo. **HABITAT AND HABITS** Occurs in wooded areas and most active at dusk. Somewhat like evening browns *Melanitis*, found at rest in undergrowth. Flight rapid for short distances when disturbed. Wings closed at rest and adults feed on overripe fruits. Unusual in that many eggs are laid together, not just a single egg as in most butterflies. Caterpillars feed on Hedge Bamboo *Bambusa multiplex*, Buddha's-belly Bamboo *B. tuldoides*, *B. ventricosa*, Hind's Cane *Pseudosasa* (*Arundinaria*) *hindsii*, *Oligostachyum* (*Arundinaria*) *shiuyingianum* and Bush Bamboo *Schizostachyum dumetorum* in grass (Poaceae) family. Adults seen year round.

Male

Female

NYMPHALIDAE

Common Evening Brown ■ *Melanitis leda* 暮眼蝶 WS 60–70mm

DESCRIPTION Medium-sized brown. Brown, somewhat variable but generally paler than Dark Evening Brown (below), especially in wet-season form. Larger eye-spots than in Dark. Distinguished from *Ypthima* ring butterflies by larger size, falcate forewings that 'hook' near apex, short wing-tail and different behaviour. Sexes similar. **DISTRIBUTION** Uncommon in HKI, NT and Lantau. Otherwise found widely in the Old World, from Sub-Saharan Africa and Indian Ocean islands, through India, to China and Japan, through SE Asia to Australia, all the way to Tahiti. **HABITAT AND HABITS** Occurs in wooded areas, usually at lower elevation than Dark. By day found resting in undergrowth, only taking short flights when disturbed. Becomes more active at dusk, with short, erratic flights in more open areas. Wings closed at rest. Adults feed on tree sap and overripe fruits. Caterpillars feed on Itchgrass *Rottboellia cochinchinensis*, *Microstegium ciliatum*, Scented Top *Capillipedium parviflorum*, *Digitaria* grass and Glutene-rice Grass *Apluda mutica* in grass (Poaceae) family. Adults seen year round.

Dry-season form

Wet-season form

Dark Evening Brown ■ *Melanitis phedima* 睇暮眼蝶 WS 65–75mm

DESCRIPTION Medium-sized brown. Dark brown, darker and redder than Common Evening Brown (above), with small eye-spots. Varies slightly between wet- and dry-season forms. Sexes similar. **DISTRIBUTION** Fairly common in HKI and NT; uncommon in Lantau. Otherwise found from India to central and southern China and Japan, through mainland SE Asia to Borneo. **HABITAT AND HABITS** Occurs in wooded areas, and can be found at higher elevation than Common. By day found resting in undergrowth, only taking short flights when disturbed. Becomes more active at dusk, with short, erratic flights in more open areas. Wings closed at rest. Adults feed on tree sap and overripe fruits. Caterpillars feed on Palmgrass *Setaria palmifolia*, Nepalese Broom Grass *Thysanolaena latifolia*, *Microstegium ciliatum*, *Ischaemum* grass and Scented Top *Capillipedium parviflorum* in grass (Poaceae) family. Adults seen year round.

▪ NYMPHALIDAE ▪

Dark-branded Bushbrown ▪ *Mycalesis mineus* 小眉眼蝶 WS 45–50mm

DESCRIPTION Medium-sized brown. Brown above with large eye-spot. Also brown below, with some variability and striking seasonal changes in appearance. Wet-season form has vertical cream line separating brown inner half from several eye-spots on outer half. Much duller in dry-season form. All forms separated from similar South China Bushbrown (opposite) by smoothly rounded forewing apex, not 'cut' or chamfered. Sexes similar, but female duller than male. **DISTRIBUTION** Common in HKI, NT and Lantau. Otherwise found from India and southern China, through mainland SE Asia, to Borneo and the Philippines. **HABITAT AND HABITS** Occurs in wooded areas and shady secondary growth. Active by day; often seen resting on forest floor or flying in slow, erratic fashion near the ground. Wings closed at rest. Adults feed on tree sap, overripe fruits and animal dung. Caterpillars feed on Nepalese Broom Grass *Thysanolaena latifolia*, *Microstegium ciliatum*, Goose Grass *Eleusine indica*, *Pogonatherum crinitum*, Sasagrass *Lophatherum gracile* and Native Rice Grass *Leersia hexandra* in grass (Poaceae) family. Adults seen year round.

Wet-season form

Dry-season form

86

NYMPHALIDAE

South China Bushbrown ■ *Mycalesis mucianus (zonata)* 平頂眉眼蝶
WS 45–50mm

DESCRIPTION
Medium-sized brown. Brown above with large eye-spot. Also brown below, with some variability and striking seasonal changes in appearance. Wet-season form has vertical cream line separating brown inner half from several eye-spots on outer half. Much duller in dry-season form. All forms distinguished from similar Dark-branded Bushbrown (opposite) by 'cut' or chamfered, not smoothly rounded, forewing apex. Sexes similar. **DISTRIBUTION** Common in HKI, NT and Lantau. Otherwise generally restricted to southeastern mainland China and Taiwan. **HABITAT AND HABITS** Occurs in wooded areas and shady secondary growth, including higher areas than Dark-branded. Active by day; often seen resting on forest floor or flying in slow, erratic fashion near the ground. Wings closed at rest. Adults feed on tree sap, overripe fruits and animal dung. Caterpillar host plants not well known, but known to feed on *Microstegium ciliatum* and other plants in grass (Poaceae) family. Adults seen year round.

Wet-season form

Dry-season form

◾ NYMPHALIDAE ◾

Common Five-Ring ◾ *Ypthima baldus* 矍眼蝶 WS 35–45mm

DESCRIPTION Relatively small brown, one of two five-rings in HK. Brown above with one forewing eye-spot and two hindwing eye-spots. Brown below; wet-season form has four medium and two small hindwing eye-spots, the front two not in line with the other four. Dry-season form lacks hindwing eye-spots below. Sexes similar. **DISTRIBUTION** Common overall. Uncommon in HKI and Lantau; common in NT. Otherwise found from India and southern China, through mainland SE Asia, to Borneo and the Philippines. **HABITAT AND HABITS** Occurs in grassy areas, especially near shrubby woodland. Active by day. Flight when disturbed weak and low. Wings closed at rest except when basking. Adults sip nectar. Caterpillar host plants not well understood, but known to feed on *Microstegium ciliatum*, *Pogonatherum crinitum* and other plants in grass (Poaceae) family. Adults seen year round.

Wet-season form

Dry-season form

NYMPHALIDAE

Straight Five-Ring ▪ *Ypthima lisandra* 黎桑矍眼蝶 WS 35–40mm

DESCRIPTION Small brown, one of two five-rings in HK. Brown above with no (male) or one (female) forewing eye-spots and two smaller hindwing eye-spots. Brown below, with four medium and two small hindwing eye-spots, forming fairly smooth arc. Dry-season form darker. **DISTRIBUTION** Uncommon in HKI, NT and Lantau. Otherwise found from southern China, through mainland SE Asia. **HABITAT AND HABITS** Occurs in grassy areas, especially near scrub or woodland. Active by day. Flight when disturbed weak and low. Wings closed at rest except when basking. Adults sip nectar. Caterpillars mainly feed on Pacific Island Silvergrass *Miscanthus floridulus* in grass (Poaceae) family. Adults seen year round.

Male

Female

Common Four-Ring ▪ *Ypthima praenubila* 前霧矍眼蝶 WS 55–60mm

DESCRIPTION Medium-sized brown, one of two four-rings in HK. Brown above with one forewing eye-spot and one (plus two tiny) hindwing eye-spots. Also brown below, with three hindwing eye-spots (plus one tiny spot in female). Distinguished from False Four-Ring (p. 90) by forewing eye-spot pattern. Common has one medium-sized forewing eye-spot above surrounded by dark brown, while False has one large eye-spot surrounded by lighter grey. Common also larger, has different pattern of dark brown forewing shading below and has two additional tiny hindwing eye-spots above. Local ranges in HK do not typically overlap. **DISTRIBUTION** Uncommon in HKI and NT; not seen in Lantau. Otherwise restricted to central and southern China. **HABITAT AND HABITS** Occurs in wooded areas. Active by day. Flight fairly strong. Wings closed at rest except when basking. Adults sip nectar. Caterpillars feed on *Pogonatherum crinitum* and other plants in grass (Poaceae) family. Adults only seen May and early June.

■ NYMPHALIDAE ■

False Four-Ring ■ *Ypthima imitans* 擬四眼矍眼蝶 WS 40–45mm

DESCRIPTION Medium-sized brown, one of two four-rings in HK. Brown above with no (male) or one (female) forewing eye-spots and one hindwing eye-spot. Brown below, with three hindwing eye-spots. See Common Four-Ring (p. 89) for more detail. **DISTRIBUTION** Rare. Not seen in HKI and NT; rare in Lantau. Otherwise restricted to southern China. **HABITAT AND HABITS** Occurs in wooded areas. Active by day. Flight fairly strong for this genus, but does not fly far. Wings closed at rest except when basking. Adults sip nectar. Caterpillar host plants not well understood in HK, but known to feed on *Microstegium ciliatum* in grass (Poaceae) family. Adults seen May–Sep. Previously referred to as *Ypthima motschulskyi imitans*.

Male

Female

Small Three-Ring ■ *Ypthima norma* 罕矍眼蝶 WS 30–35mm

DESCRIPTION Small brown, the sole three-ring in HK. Brown above with one forewing eye-spot, and no (male) or one (female) hindwing eye-spots. Brown below, with three small hindwing eye-spots (reduced or absent in dry season). **DISTRIBUTION** Uncommon. Not seen in HKI and Lantau; fairly common in NT. Otherwise found from India to southern China, through mainland SE Asia, to eastern Indonesia and the Philippines. **HABITAT AND HABITS** Occurs on grassy hill slopes. Active by day. Flight weak and low to the ground. Wings closed at rest except when basking. Adults sip nectar. Caterpillar host plants not well understood in HK, but known to feed on *Microstegium ciliatum* in grass (Poaceae) family. Adults seen year round.

Dry-season form

◼ NYMPHALIDAE ◼

Banded Treebrown ◼ *Lethe confusa* 白帶黛眼蝶 WS 55mm

DESCRIPTION Medium-sized brown with broad diagonal forewing-band. Distinct hindwing eye-spots below. Sexes similar, though female less reddish below. DISTRIBUTION Common in HKI, NT and Lantau. Otherwise found from central and southern China, through mainland SE Asia. HABITAT AND HABITS Occurs in woodland edges and along paths. Active by day. Flight strong, but often found basking, returning to a favoured perch after being disturbed. Wings closed at rest. Adults feed on tree sap and overripe fruits. Caterpillars feed on Pacific Island Silvergrass *Miscanthus floridulus*, Chinese Silvergrass *M. sinensis*, Scented Top *Capillipedium parviflorum* and *Microstegium ciliatum* in grass (Poaceae) family. Adults seen year round.

Bamboo Treebrown ◼ *Lethe europa* 長紋黛眼蝶 WS 60mm

DESCRIPTION Medium-sized brown. Similar to Banded Treebrown (above), except male lacks white forewing-band above and in both sexes hindwing eye-spots below not clear. DISTRIBUTION Uncommon. Fairly common in HKI; uncommon in NT and Lantau. Otherwise found from India to southern China, through mainland SE Asia, to Borneo and the Philippines. HABITAT AND HABITS Occurs near bamboo in wooded areas. Active by day. Flight strong, and can be territorial. Wings closed at rest. Adults feed on tree sap, overripe fruits and animal dung. Caterpillars feed on Buddha's-belly Bamboo *Bambusa tuldoides*, Hedge Bamboo *B. multiplex* and *Microstegium ciliatum* in grass (Poaceae) family. Adults seen year round.

Male

Female

▪ NYMPHALIDAE ▪

Common Treebrown ▪ *Lethe rohria* 波紋黛眼蝶 WS 60–70mm

DESCRIPTION Medium-sized brown. Similar to Bamboo Treebrown (p. 91), except hindwing-underside base has a wavy pattern, and top hindwing-underside eye-spot is clearer. Female darker but sexes similar. **DISTRIBUTION** Rare. Not seen in HKI and Lantau; uncommon in NT. Otherwise found from India to southern China, through mainland SE Asia, to Borneo and the Philippines. **HABITAT AND HABITS** Occurs in woodland edges, usually in shade. Active by day. Flight moderately strong. Wings closed at rest. Adults feed on tree sap, overripe fruits and animal dung. Caterpillars feed on Scented Top *Capillipedium parviflorum*, Glutene-rice Grass *Apluda mutica* and *Microstegium ciliatum* in grass (Poaceae) family. Adults seen year round.

Angled Red Forester ▪ *Lethe chandica* 曲紋黛眼蝶 WS 60–70mm

DESCRIPTION Medium-sized brown. Dark reddish-brown, generally plainer than other *Lethe*. Female has white half-band on forewing-underside. **DISTRIBUTION** Uncommon. Not seen in HKI and Lantau; fairly common in NT. Otherwise found from India to central and southern China, through mainland SE Asia, to Borneo and the Philippines. **HABITAT AND HABITS** Occurs in shaded wooded areas and near bamboo. Active by day. Flight moderately strong. Wings closed at rest. Adults thought to feed on tree sap, overripe fruits and animal dung. Caterpillar host plants not widely known, but probably include bamboo plants in grass (Poaceae) family. Adults seen Feb–Dec.

Male

Female

92

NYMPHALIDAE

Black-spotted Labyrinth ■ *Neope muirheadii* 蒙鏈蔭眼蝶 WS 60–70mm

Wet-season form

Dry-season form

DESCRIPTION Medium-sized brown, with vertical cream line below separating inner and outer halves of wings. Similar to bushbrowns, but larger, and inner half of underside has intricate markings. Dry-season pattern more muted. **DISTRIBUTION** Uncommon. Not seen in HKI and Lantau; fairly common in NT. Otherwise found from central and southern China, through mainland SE Asia. **HABITAT AND HABITS** Occurs in shaded wooded areas and near bamboo. Active by day. Flight brief and strong when disturbed, often settling on the ground or on tree trunk. Wings closed at rest. Adults feed on tree sap, overripe fruits and animal dung. Unusual in that many eggs are laid together, not just a single egg as in most butterflies. Caterpillars feed on Black Bamboo *Phyllostachys nigra*, Buddha's-belly Bamboo *Bambusa tuldoides*, Hedge Bamboo *B. multiplex* and Hinds' Cane *Pseudosasa* (*Arundinaria*) *hindsii* in grass (Poaceae) family. Adults seen Feb–Sep.

Yellow Coster ■ *Telchinia* (*Acraea*) *issoria* 苧麻珍蝶 WS 60–70mm

DESCRIPTION Distinctive, medium-sized butterfly. Yellowish-orange with black veins, especially below. Female markings slightly darker. **DISTRIBUTION** Uncommon. Not seen in HKI and Lantau; uncommon in NT. Otherwise found from India to central and southern China, through mainland SE Asia. Locally in western Indonesia. **HABITAT AND HABITS** Occurs in openings in wooded areas and along streams. Flight weak. Often seen at rest. Active by day. Adults sip nectar. Host plants in HK not well known. Elsewhere caterpillars reported to feed on False Nettles *Boehmeria* and *Pouzolzia* in nettle (Urticaceae) family. Adults seen Apr–Sep.

◾ NYMPHALIDAE ◾

Red Lacewing Butterfly ◾ *Cethosia biblis* 紅鋸蛺蝶 WS 70mm

Male

DESCRIPTION Medium-sized butterfly with serrated wing margins. Male reddish-orange above with black margins. Female duller orange above. Below both sexes have dazzling pattern of zigzag black and white markings, interspersed with orange bands.
DISTRIBUTION Uncommon. Rare in HKI and NT; uncommon in Lantau. Otherwise found from India to southern China, through mainland SE Asia, to Borneo and the Philippines. **HABITAT AND HABITS** Occurs in coastal shrubland and wooded areas. Male ranges widely, and may be seen flying over hills. Female stays much closer to colonies near host plants. Flight fairly slow, and male (which mimics toxic Plain Tiger Butterfly, p. 72) conspicuous. Active by day, and adults sip nectar. Caterpillars feed on *Passiflora cochinchinensis* in passionflower (Passifloraceae) family. Adults seen Mar–Dec.

Male

Grey form female

NYMPHALIDAE

Tropical Fritillary
Argynnis (Argyreus) hyperbius 斐豹蛺蝶 WS 70–80mm

DESCRIPTION Medium-sized butterfly. Male orange above with black spots, scalloped wing-margins and thicker black trailing hindwing-edge than Common Leopard (p. 96). Tropical Fritillary larger and significantly different below, with dark orange forewing and contrasting hindwing pattern. Female orange above with black spots, black wing apex and white diagonal bar, mimicking toxic Plain Tiger Butterfly (p. 72). Underside pattern similar to male and strikingly different from Plain Tiger. **DISTRIBUTION** Fairly common in HKI and Lantau; common in NT. Otherwise found from India, to central and northern China, Korea and Japan, through mainland SE Asia, to Indonesia and the Philippines. **HABITAT AND HABITS** Occurs in open secondary habitats, often resting on the ground, then making fast, erratic flights. Males hilltop and can be difficult to approach. Active by day, and adults sip nectar. Caterpillars feed on Long-sepaled Violet *Viola inconspicua* in violet (Violaceae) family. Adults seen year round.

Male

Female

Female

Female

▪ NYMPHALIDAE ▪

Common Leopard ▪ *Phalanta phalantha* 珐蛱蝶 WS 55–60mm

DESCRIPTION Medium-sized butterfly. Similar to male Tropical Fritillary (p. 95): orange with black spots on wing-margins, brighter in wet-season form. Common Leopard smaller with smaller black spots and narrower black hindwing-margin. Margins not scalloped. Underside similar to upperside, with addition of light purple shading on hindwing-margins. This contrasts with Tropical Fritillary, which has strikingly different pattern below. Sexes similar. **DISTRIBUTION** Rare in HKI, NT and Lantau. Otherwise found from Sub-Saharan Africa and India, to southern China, through mainland SE Asia, to the Philippines and northern Australia. **HABITAT AND HABITS** Sun-loving and migratory species that generally avoids Asian monsoon season. Occurs in open, shrubby areas, where male can be territorial. Flight brisk. Active by day, and adults sip nectar. Caterpillars feed on Chinese Scolopia *Scolopia chinensis* and ornamental Weeping Willow *Salix babylonica* in willow (Salicaceae) family. Adults seen Oct–Jan.

Rustic ▪ *Cupha erymanthis* 黃襟蛱蝶 WS 50–60mm

DESCRIPTION Medium-sized butterfly. Orangish-brown above with buffy forewing-patch and black wing-tip. Buffy-brown below, with row of black spots in centre of hindwing. Sexes similar. **DISTRIBUTION** Common in HKI, NT and Lantau. Otherwise found from India to southern China, through mainland SE Asia, to Borneo and the Philippines. **HABITAT AND HABITS** Occurs in woodland edges. Males establish territory in shrubs near host plant and sally forth on short flights to chase away intruders. Flight moderate. Active by day, and adults sip nectar. Caterpillars feed on Kwangtung Scolopia *Scolopia saeva*, Chinese Scolopia *S. chinensis* and *Homalium cochinchinense* in willow (Salicaceae) family. Also feeds on ornamental Weeping Willow *Salix babylonica*. Adults seen year round.

NYMPHALIDAE

Short Banded Sailer ■ *Phaedyma columella* 柱菲蛺蝶 WS 50mm

DESCRIPTION Medium-sized butterfly. Similar to *Neptis* sailers, but above has distinctive 2x2 forewing spots (two groups of two spots on each wing). Forewing cell-end spot distinctively blunt. Similar pattern below, and often quite orangish with a few differences from *Neptis*. Sexes similar. **DISTRIBUTION** Fairly common. Common in HKI and Lantau; fairly common in NT. Otherwise found from India to southern China, through mainland SE Asia, to Borneo and the Philippines. **HABITAT AND HABITS** Occurs in wooded areas. Sailing flight near the ground with long glides on flat wings. Active by day; wings held flat at rest. Adults sip nectar and caterpillars feed on Hedge Sageretia *Sageretia thea* in buckthorn (Rhamnacae) family, Reevesia *Reevesia thyrsoidea* and Lance-leaved Sterculia *Sterculia lanceolata* in mallow (Malvaceae) family, Yellow Cow Wood *Cratoxylum cochinchinense* in St John's wort (Hypericaceae) family and *Tadehagi triquetrum* in legume (Fabaceae) family. Adults seen Mar–Nov.

◾ NYMPHALIDAE ◾

Common Sailer ◾ *Neptis hylas* 中環蛺蝶 WS 55mm

DESCRIPTION Medium-sized butterfly, dark brown above with three horizontal white bands. White and orange-brown banding below. White banding slightly wider in wet-season form. Above, distinguished from Southern Sullied Sailer (opposite) by forewing cell-end spot that is fully detached from cell bar. Below, narrow black edging to central white band. Also, whereas white band of Cream-spotted Sailer (p. 100) widens towards costa (upper edge), in Common this band does not widen. Sexes similar. **DISTRIBUTION** Common in HKI, NT and Lantau. Otherwise found from India to southern China, through mainland SE Asia, to Borneo and the Philippines. **HABITAT AND HABITS** Occurs in wooded and shrubby areas with low vegetation. Sailing flight near the ground with long glides on flat wings. Active by day; wings held flat at rest. Adults drawn to damp patches on the ground, flower nectar and tree sap. Caterpillars feed on Beach Bean *Canavalia rosea*, Streaked Rattlepod *Crotalaria pallida*, Asian Ticktrefoil *Grona heterocarpos*, *G. reticulata*, *Tadehagi triquetrum* and Tropical Kudzu *Neustanthus* (*Pueraria*) *phaseoloides* in legume (Fabaceae) family, Nettle Tree *Trema tomentosa* in hackberry (Cannabaceae) family and Paper Mulberry *Broussonetia papyrifera* in mulberry and fig (Moraceae) family. Adults seen year round, with dry-season form visible Nov–Apr.

NYMPHALIDAE

Southern Sullied Sailer ■ *Neptis clinia* 珂環蛺蝶 WS 45–50mm

DESCRIPTION Smaller than Common Sailer (opposite), but quite similar. Dark brown above with three horizontal white bands. Underside alternating white and orange bands. Above, distinguished from Common by forewing cell-end spot not fully detached from cell bar. Below, lack of narrow black edging to central white band. Southern Sullied underside bands more brown (v orange-brown). Unlike in Cream-spotted Sailer (p. 100), central underside white band does not widen. Also, in Southern Sullied the three forewing apical white spots (above and below) curve in usual way, while in Cream-spotted they curve out, towards apex. Sexes similar. **DISTRIBUTION** Common in HKI; fairly common in NT and Lantau. Otherwise found from India to southern China, through mainland SE Asia, to Borneo. **HABITAT AND HABITS** Occurs in wooded and shrubby areas with low vegetation. Sailing flight near the ground with long glides on flat wings. Active by day; wings held flat at rest. Adults drawn to damp patches on the ground, flower nectar and tree sap. Caterpillars feed on Bentham's Rosewood *Dalbergia benthamii* in legume (Fabaceae) family. Adults seen Apr–Aug.

◾ NYMPHALIDAE ◾

Cream-spotted Sailer ◾ *Neptis soma* 娑環蛺蝶 WS 50–55mm

DESCRIPTION Medium-sized butterfly. Dark brown above with three horizontal white bands. Alternating white and brown bands below. Differs from Southern Sullied Sailer (p. 99) by widening of central underside white band. In Cream-spotted white band widens towards costa (upper edge), but in Southern Sullied it does not widen. In Southern Sullied three forewing apical white spots (above and below) curve in the usual way, while in Cream-spotted they curve out, towards apex. Sexes similar. **DISTRIBUTION** Rare. Not seen in HKI and Lantau; rare, mainly around Kadoorie Farm, in NT. Otherwise found from India to central and southern China, through mainland SE Asia. **HABITAT AND HABITS** Occurs in wooded areas at higher elevations. Sailing flight near the ground with long glides on flat wings. Active by day; wings held flat at rest. Adults sip nectar. Caterpillar host plants not well known in HK, though in India larvae feed on *Sterculia* plants in mallow (Malvaceae) family. Adults seen Mar–Oct.

NYMPHALIDAE

Sullied Brown Sailer ■ *Neptis nata* 娜環蛺蝶 WS 45–50mm

DESCRIPTION Smaller than Common Sailer (p. 98), but similar. Blacker above, with narrower white horizontal bands, both above and below. Forewing cell-end spot fully detached from cell bar. Sexes similar. **DISTRIBUTION** Recent colonist to HK, since 2017 or so. Now uncommon. Uncommon in HKI; fairly common in NT; rare in Lantau. Otherwise found from India to southern China, through mainland SE Asia, to Borneo. **HABITAT AND HABITS** Occurs in wooded and shrubby areas with low vegetation. Sailing flight near the ground with long glides on flat wings. Active by day; wings held flat at rest. One of the only sailers in HK in which males display hilltopping and other territorial behaviour. Adults drawn to damp patches on the ground, flower nectar and tree sap. Caterpillars feed on Nettle Tree *Trema tomentosa* in hackberry (Cannabaceae) family. Adults seen Mar–Dec.

Plain Sailer ■ *Neptis cartica* 卡環蛺蝶 WS 45–50mm

DESCRIPTION Medium-sized butterfly, similar to Sullied Brown Sailer (above), but in Plain forewing cell-end spot incompletely detached from cell bar. White bands tend to be slightly broader, and dark, plain forewing apex with little or no white spotting, unlike in most sailers. Sexes similar. **DISTRIBUTION** Rarely seen in HK, since 2019 or so. Not seen in HKI and Lantau; rare in NT. Otherwise found from India to southern China and mainland SE Asia. **HABITAT AND HABITS** Occurs in wooded and shrubby areas with low vegetation. Sailing flight near the ground with long glides on flat wings. Active by day; wings held flat at rest. Adults sip nectar. Caterpillar host plants not well known. Adults seen Apr–Dec.

■ NYMPHALIDAE ■

Small Yellow Sailer ■ *Neptis miah* 彌環蛺蝶 WS 50mm

DESCRIPTION Medium-sized butterfly. Orange and black striped above, with three horizontal and one diagonal orange stripes. Wing apex dark. Orange and dark brown-striped below. Narrower orange bands above than in female Common Lascar and Colour Sergeant (below and opposite). Also lacks thin orange forewing marginal line of Common Lascar and orange apex spot of Colour Sergeant female. From below, Common Lascar orange banding obscured by brown markings, and Colour Sergeant bands wider. Sexes similar. **DISTRIBUTION** Uncommon in HK. Rare in HKI; uncommon in NT; not seen in Lantau. Otherwise found from India to central and southern China, through mainland SE Asia, to Borneo. **HABITAT AND HABITS** Occurs in wooded areas. Sailing flight near the ground with long glides on flat wings. Active by day; wings held flat at rest. Adults sip nectar. Caterpillar host plants not well known. Adults seen Mar–Dec.

Common Lascar ■ *Pantoporia hordonia* 金蟠蛺蝶 WS 35–50mm

DESCRIPTION Smaller than *Neptis* sailers. Has broader orange bands above than in Small Yellow Sailer (above), alongside thin orange line along forewing-margin. From below, orange banding obscured by brown markings. Sexes similar. **DISTRIBUTION** Uncommon overall. Uncommon in HKI and NT; not seen in Lantau. Otherwise found from India to southern China, through mainland SE Asia to Borneo. **HABITAT AND HABITS** Occurs in wooded areas, especially more open sections. Flight weak, generally gliding around host plant. Active by day; wings held flat at rest. Adults rest often on leaves and flowers, and visit damp patches. Caterpillars feed on Monkey-Pod *Archidendron clypearia* and *Albizia corniculata* in legume (Fabaceae) family. Adults seen Mar–Dec.

NYMPHALIDAE

Colour Sergeant ■ *Athyma nefte* 相思帶蛺蝶 WS 55–65mm

DESCRIPTION Larger than *Neptis* and *Phaedyma* sailers. Male black above and dark brown below, with three white bands and orange patch at forewing apex. Female black above with three horizontal orange bands, one diagonal orange band and one orange spot at apex. Similar to Orange Staff Sergeant (p. 104), but orange apex patch larger. Both sexes have light bands below. Common Jester (p. 120) similar but with short wing-tail, and lacks Colour Sergeant's stripes below. **DISTRIBUTION** Common in HKI, NT and Lantau. Otherwise found from India to southern China, through mainland SE Asia, to Borneo. **HABITAT AND HABITS** Occurs in wooded areas. Males congregate at hilltops, perching on shrubs in their territories and chasing off potential rivals. Flight strong; wings held flat at rest. Active by day. Caterpillars feed on abacus *Glochidion* plants in leaf-flower (Phyllanthaceae) family, especially Hairy-fruited Abacus Plant *G. eriocarpum*, *G. puberum* and *G. wrightii*. Adults seen year round, especially July–Aug.

Male

Male

Female

Female

103

▪ Nymphalidae ▪

Orange Staff Sergeant ▪ *Athyma cama* 雙色帶蛺蝶 WS 55–65mm

Left: female, right: male

DESCRIPTION Larger than *Neptis* and *Phaedyma* sailers. Male black above and dark brown below, with one white band and orange patch at forewing apex. Female black above with three orange bands. Similar to Colour Sergeant (p. 103), but orange apex patch smaller in Orange Staff Sergeant. Both sexes have light bands below. Common Jester (p. 120) similar but with short wing-tail, and lacks stripes below. **DISTRIBUTION** Rare overall. Not seen in HKI and Lantau; rare in NT. Otherwise found from India to southern China, through mainland SE Asia, to Borneo. **HABITAT AND HABITS** Occurs in mountainous areas, where males are aggressively territorial. Flight strong; wings held flat at rest. Active by day. Caterpillars feed on abacus *Glochidion* plants in leaf-flower (Phyllanthaceae) family. Adults seen Nov–May; one of the few butterflies most commonly seen in winter. **Note** Photo at top and bottom left taken in northern Guangdong Province.

Left: female, right: male

Male

NYMPHALIDAE

Common Sergeant ◾ *Athyma perius* 玄珠帶蛺蝶 WS 65mm

DESCRIPTION Larger than *Neptis* and *Phaedyma* sailers. Black with three white bands above. A few thin white abdominal bands, and three fairly square white dots in first white band on each wing. Below, banded orange and white, with row of black dots inside last white band. Sexes similar. DISTRIBUTION Uncommon. Not seen in HKI; uncommon in NT and Lantau. Otherwise found from India to southern China, through mainland SE Asia, to Borneo and the Philippines. HABITAT AND HABITS Occurs in shrubby areas. Flight strong, and males hilltop. Active by day; wings held flat at rest. Adults take nectar, and caterpillars feed on several species of abacus *Glochidion* plant in leaf-flower (Phyllanthaceae) family. Adults seen Mar–Dec.

Blackvein Sergeant ◾ *Athyma ranga* 離斑帶蛺蝶 WS 60–70mm

DESCRIPTION Larger than *Neptis* and *Phaedyma* sailers. Fairly distinctive black and white butterfly. Male black above with two broad white stripes and white patches. White underneath with black stripes and veining. Female similar but with more white above and below. DISTRIBUTION Uncommon. Rare in HKI; uncommon in NT and Lantau. Otherwise found from India to central and southern China, through mainland SE Asia. HABITAT AND HABITS Occurs in wooded areas. Flight strong, and males hilltop. Active by day; wings held flat at rest. Adults mainly feed on overripe fruits and animal faeces. Caterpillars known to feed on Chinese Flowering Ash *Fraxinus insularis* and Fragrant Osmanthus *Osmanthus fragrans* in olive (Oleaceae) family. Adults seen year round.

Male *Female*

■ NYMPHALIDAE ■

Staff Sergeant ■ *Athyma selenophora* 新月帶蛺蝶 WS 55–65mm

DESCRIPTION Larger than *Neptis* and *Phaedyma* sailers. Male black above and dark brown below, with white band and small orange highlights on forewing. Female black above with three white bands, a similar pattern to sailers. Sergeants' (*Athyma*) wings generally rounder (less elongated horizontally) than those of sailers. Female has pale abdominal band in line with middle white wing-band. First band (near head) has unusual, elongated dash laterally, and two compact spots medially – different pattern than in similar butterflies. Both sexes have light bands below. **DISTRIBUTION** Fairly common in HKI, NT and Lantau. Otherwise found from India to central and southern China, through mainland SE Asia, to Borneo and the Philippines. **HABITAT AND HABITS** Occurs in wooded areas, where both sexes choose preferred perches to which they return often. Flight strong; wings held flat at rest. Active by day. Adults seldom seen sipping nectar, but do feed on overripe fruits. Caterpillars feed on Chinese Buttonbush *Adina pilulifera*, Splash-of-White *Mussaenda pubescens* and *M. erosa* in coffee (Rubiaceae) family. Adults seen year round, especially July–Aug.

Male

Male

Female

Female

■ NYMPHALIDAE ■

Five-dot Sergeant ■ *Limenitis (Parathyma) sulpitia* 殘鍔線蛺蝶 WS 60–70mm

DESCRIPTION Larger and rounder than *Neptis* and *Phaedyma* sailers. Black with three white bands above. In first band, forewing cell-end spot often, but not always, attached to cell bar, forming complete line. Orange and white bands underneath, with five black spots at hindwing-base. Sexes similar. DISTRIBUTION Fairly common in HKI, NT and Lantau. Otherwise restricted to central and southern China. HABITAT AND HABITS Occurs in gardens, secondary growth and wooded areas. Often basks in sunshine with open wings. Can be territorial, positioned a few metres above the ground and chasing off intruders. Active by day. Adults mainly feed on nectar and overripe fruits. Caterpillars feed on several species of honeysuckle *Lonicera* in honeysuckle (Caprifoliaceae) family. Adults seen Feb–Nov.

White Commodore ■ *Parasarpa dudu* Y紋俳蛺蝶 WS 65–70mm

DESCRIPTION Distinctive, medium to large butterfly. Male dark brown above, with pointed forewing and broad, diagonal white band on each side. Similar pattern below, but lighter. Female lighter overall. DISTRIBUTION Uncommon overall. Uncommon in HKI and Lantau; fairly common in NT. Otherwise found from India to southern China, through mainland SE Asia. HABITAT AND HABITS Occurs in wooded areas, especially in highlands, where males hilltop. Rapid, swooping flight. Can be aggressive when flying around its chosen territory, and has been seen chasing off swallows (birds). Active by day; wings held flat at rest. Adults mainly feed on nectar and overripe fruits. Caterpillars feed on honeysuckles *Lonicera* in honeysuckle (Caprifoliaceae) family. Adults seen Feb–Nov.

◾ NYMPHALIDAE ◾

Commander ◾ *Moduza procris* 穆蛺蝶 WS 70mm

DESCRIPTION Large, distinctive butterfly. Orange and brown with large diagonal white stripe on each side. Sexes similar. **DISTRIBUTION** Uncommon. Rare in HKI; fairly common in NT; not seen in Lantau. Otherwise found from India to southern China, through mainland SE Asia, to Borneo. **HABITAT AND HABITS** Occurs in openings in wooded areas and along streams. Strong flight, though does not usually fly far. Active by day, when it basks in the sun with wings spread flat. Males hilltop and adults feed on nectar and overripe fruits. Host plants in HK not well known. Elsewhere caterpillars reported to feed on *Grewia* (*Microcos*) *nervosa* (*paniculata*) in mallow (Malvaceae) family and *Mussaenda* in coffee (Rubiaceae) family. Adults seen Apr–Nov.

Common Baron ◾ *Euthalia aconthea* 矛翠蛺蝶 WS 65mm

DESCRIPTION Medium-sized butterfly. Male forewing pointed, golden-brown to dark brown above with a few grey spots. Brown and grey below. Female forewing more rounded. Caterpillar like Common Archduke's (p. 112). **DISTRIBUTION** Uncommon in HKI and NT; rare in Lantau. Otherwise found from India to southern China, through mainland SE Asia, to Borneo and the Philippines. **HABITAT AND HABITS** Occurs in wooded areas, with both sexes alert and flying rapidly with clipped wingbeats only slightly below the horizontal. Active by day and may be seen perched at mid-levels, with male taking moisture from the ground. Wings held flat at rest. Adults do not commonly sip nectar; mainly attracted to hanging or fallen fruits. Caterpillars feed on Indian Mango *Mangifera indica* in cashew (Anacardiaceae) family and Cinnamon Mistletoe *Scurrula parasitica* in showy mistletoe (Loranthaceae) family. Adults seen May–Sep.

NYMPHALIDAE

Gaudy Baron ■ *Euthalia lubentina* 紅斑翠蛺蝶 WS 65mm

DESCRIPTION Medium-sized butterfly. Male forewing pointed, greenish-grey above with white spots. Distinctive carmine-red hindwing-spots. Brown and carmine below. Female forewing more rounded – greenish-grey above and with diagonal white band above and below. Hindwing has carmine red spots. Caterpillar like Common Archduke's (p. 112).
DISTRIBUTION Uncommon overall. Uncommon in HKI; fairly common in NT; not seen in Lantau. Otherwise found from India to southern China, through mainland SE Asia, to Borneo and the Philippines. **HABITAT AND HABITS** Occurs in woodland, with both sexes alert and flying rapidly in canopy. Active by day; wings held flat at rest. Adults do not commonly sip nectar; mainly attracted to hanging or fallen fruits. Caterpillars feed on Common Chinese Mistletoe *Macrosolen cochinchinensis* and Cinnamon Mistletoe *Scurrula parasitica* in showy mistletoe (Loranthaceae) family. Adults seen Mar–Oct.

Male

Male

Female

Female

◾ NYMPHALIDAE ◾

White-edged Blue Baron ◾ *Euthalia phemius* 尖翅翠蛺蝶 WS 65mm

DESCRIPTION Medium-sized butterfly. Male forewing pointed, brownish-black above with thin white costal lines. Hindwing has thick blue patch, shining white along trailing margin. Brown below. Female forewing more rounded, dark brown above with diagonal white band above and below. Lighter brown below. Caterpillar like Common Archduke's (p. 112). **DISTRIBUTION** Fairly common in HKI, NT and Lantau. Otherwise found from India to southern China, through mainland SE Asia. **HABITAT AND HABITS** Occurs in woodland, with female typically in canopy and seldom seen. Males often perch on forest floor, sipping moisture from damp areas. Active by day. Glides near forest floor, flapping only slightly below the horizonal in a clipped flight. Wings held flat at rest. Adults do not sip nectar but can be seen on fallen fruits. Caterpillars feed on Indian Mango *Mangifera indica* in cashew (Anacardiaceae) family. Adults seen year round, especially July–Oct.

NYMPHALIDAE

Green Skirt Baron ■ *Tanaecia whiteheadi (Euthalia niepelti)* 綠裙蛺蝶
WS 60mm

DESCRIPTION Medium-sized butterfly. Male forewing pointed, black above with a few grey or light blue spots near leading edge. Hindwing has medium-width light blue band and black trailing margin. Dark brown below, plainer than related species. Female forewing more rounded. Caterpillar like Common Archduke's (p. 112). **DISTRIBUTION** Uncommon. Not seen in HKI and Lantau; fairly common in NT. Not widespread outside HK; mainly found in southeastern China. **HABITAT AND HABITS** Occurs in wooded areas, with both sexes alert and flying rapidly with clipped wingbeats only slightly below the horizontal. Active by day, with male taking moisture from the ground. Wings held flat at rest. Adults do not sip nectar and mainly attracted to hanging or fallen fruits. Caterpillar host plants not widely known. Adults seen Apr–Nov.

Angled Castor ■ *Ariadne ariadne* 波蛺蝶 WS 55–60mm

DESCRIPTION Medium-sized butterfly. Orangish-brown above and below, with wavy black lines and distinctive white spot on forewing costa. Darker below. Sexes similar. **DISTRIBUTION** Uncommon in HKI and Lantau; fairly common in NT. Otherwise found from India to southern China, through mainland SE Asia. **HABITAT AND HABITS** Occurs near villages where host plant grows. Slow flight. Active by day and wings often held closed at rest. Adults feed on nectar. Caterpillars feed on Castor Bean *Ricinus communis* in spurge (Euphorbiaceae) family. Adults seen year round.

NYMPHALIDAE

Common Archduke ◾ *Lexias pardalis* 小豹律蛺蝶 WS 85mm

DESCRIPTION Large butterfly. Male black above with orange dots along costa. Hindwing edged in bright metallic blue, with black spots along trailing margin. Rusty-brown below. Female dark brown with lemon-yellow spotting, perhaps mimicking dappled sunlight on forest floor. Caterpillars, especially later instars, remarkable – lime green and spiny, with orange dots. **DISTRIBUTION** Previously rare or absent; fairly recent colonist of HK. Now well established and common across HK. Common in HKI, NT and Lantau. Otherwise found from eastern India to southern China, through mainland SE Asia, to Borneo. **HABITAT AND HABITS** Occurs in lowland woodland edges and along paths. Active by day. Glides near forest floor, flapping only slightly below the horizonal in a clipped flight. Wings held flat at rest, slowly opening and closing. Adults sip nectar but especially fond of overripe fruits on forest floor. Caterpillars feed on Yellow Cow Wood *Cratoxylum cochinchinense* in St John's wort (Hypericacaeae) family. Adults seen year round, less commonly in winter.

Male

Male

Female

Caterpillar

112

NYMPHALIDAE

Black Prince ■ *Rohana parisatis* 羅蛺蝶 WS 45–50mm

Male

Male

Female

Female

DESCRIPTION Medium-sized butterfly. Male black above and dark below, with reddish-brown and light blue highlights. Female orangish-brown above and below; three white apical spots above and below. **DISTRIBUTION** Fairly common in HKI; uncommon in NT and Lantau. Otherwise found from India to southern China, through mainland SE Asia, to Borneo and the Philippines. **HABITAT AND HABITS** Occurs in wooded areas. Active by day and often found basking with wings flat; male on paths and female on vegetation. Can be approached closely before it flies off strongly. Adults feed on nectar and tree sap. Caterpillars feed on Philippine Hackberry *Celtis timorensis* in hackberry (Cannabaceae) family. Adults seen year round.

NYMPHALIDAE

Red Ring Skirt ■ *Hestina assimilis* 黑脈蛺蝶 WS 80–100mm

DESCRIPTION Large butterfly that mimics toxic black and white tiger butterflies. Typical form *assimilis* white with thick black vein markings and four red submarginal hindwing-spots. In spring, lighter form *nigrivena* with less black can be found alongside *assimilis*. Sexes similar. **DISTRIBUTION** Fairly common in HKI, NT and Lantau. Otherwise found across southern, central and northern China, to Korea and Japan. **HABITAT AND HABITS** Occurs in wooded areas. Flight strong and often high, at canopy level. Active by day and males sometimes hilltop. Wings held closed at rest. Adults feed on nectar and tree sap. Caterpillars feed on Chinese Hackberry *Celtis sinensis* in hackberry (Cannabaceae) family. Adults seen Apr–Dec.

assimilis

assimilis

nigrivena

nigrivena

▪ NYMPHALIDAE ▪

Courtesan ▪ *Euripus nyctelius* 芒蛺蝶 WS 55–70mm

Male

Male

Female

Female

DESCRIPTION Medium-sized butterfly with distinctive yellow eye that mimics black and white tiger (male) and black crow (female) butterflies. Male has striped pattern above and below, and short wing-tail. Female black above and below, with dark blue gloss on forewing-upperside. Similar to *Euploea* crow butterflies below, but Courtesan has yellow eyes, more regular and extensive marginal spotting and arc of clear white submarginal dots. **DISTRIBUTION** Uncommon in HKI and NT; rare in Lantau. Otherwise found from India to southern China, through mainland SE Asia, to Borneo and the Philippines. **HABITAT AND HABITS** Occurs in wooded areas. Male flight strong, but female mimics slow *Euploea* crow flight. Active by day and wings held closed at rest. Adults feed on nectar and overripe fruits. Caterpillars feed on Nettle Tree *Trema tomentosa*, Lesser Trema *T. cannabina* and Oriental Trema *T. orientale* (*orientalis*) in hackberry (Cannabaceae) family. Adults seen Feb–Nov.

NYMPHALIDAE

Eastern Courtier ■ *Sephisa chandra* 帥蛺蝶 WS 70–85mm

DESCRIPTION Striking medium to large butterfly. Male orange and black, with white apical spots. Female rarely, if ever, seen in HK, blue and white above, with one orange forewing-spot and seven orange spots below. Thought to mimic toxic day-flying moths: perhaps male model is a forester moth (Noctuidae, Agaristinae: *Episteme*) and that for female a burnet moth (Zygaenidae: *Erasmia*). **DISTRIBUTION** Rare in HKI, NT and Lantau. Otherwise found from India to southern China, through mainland SE Asia. **HABITAT AND HABITS** Occurs in wooded areas. Male flight very rapid along paths, similar to a forester moth, but female mimics slow burnet moth flight. Can be territorial, and at times tolerates close approach as it returns to favoured perches. Active by day; wings held closed at rest. Adults feed on nectar and tree sap, and visit damp ground to drink. Caterpillar host plant thought to be Ring-cupped Oak *Quercus glauca* in beech (Fagaceae) family. Adults, almost exclusively male, seen May–Oct, mainly May.

◾ NYMPHALIDAE ◾

Constable ◾ *Dichorragia nesimachus* 電蛺蝶 WS 70mm

DESCRIPTION Medium to large butterfly. Black above and below, with white 'V'-shaped markings and spots, plus blue gloss. Sexes similar. **DISTRIBUTION** Uncommon overall. Not seen in HKI; fairly common in NT; rare in Lantau. Otherwise found from India to central and southern China, Korea and Japan, through SE Asia, to Borneo and the Philippines. **HABITAT AND HABITS** Occurs in wooded areas and along trails. Can be territorial from a perch, chasing away rivals in strong flight. Active by day; wings held flat at rest. Males hilltop and adults feed on tree sap. Caterpillars feed on Stiff-leaved Meliosma *Meliosma rigida* and Ford's Meliosma *M. fordii* in sabia (Sabiaceae) family. Adults seen Mar–Oct.

Common Mapwing ◾ *Cyrestis thyodamas* 網絲蛺蝶 WS 55mm

DESCRIPTION Striking medium-sized butterfly. Cream above and below; some females more yellowish, with intricate pattern of black lines. Hindwing has some orange and blue. Sexes similar. **DISTRIBUTION** Common in HKI and NT; fairly common in Lantau. Otherwise found from India to central and southern China, to Japan, and through mainland SE Asia. **HABITAT AND HABITS** Occurs around damp patches and rotting material, along trails and around fig trees, the host plants. Active by day; wings held flat at rest, pressed to the ground or underside of a leaf. Adults feed on rotting material; rarely seen at flowers. Males visit damp sand. Caterpillars feed on Chinese Banyan *Ficus microcarpa*, Superb Fig *F. subpisocarpa* (*superba*) and Common Red-stem Fig *F. variegata* in mulberry and fig (Moraceae) family. Adults seen year round.

117

▪ NYMPHALIDAE ▪

Blue Admiral ▪ *Kaniska canace* 琉璃蛺蝶 WS 65–75mm

DESCRIPTION Medium-sized dark brown butterfly with ragged wings and diagonal blue band above. Brown below with intricate, bark-like pattern. Sexes similar. Caterpillar striking, with orange and white bands, marked black, plus branched cream spines.
DISTRIBUTION Uncommon in HKI and Lantau; fairly common in NT. Otherwise found from India to central and northern China, Korea and Japan, through mainland SE Asia, to Borneo and the Philippines. **HABITAT AND HABITS** Occurs in woodland clearings and along stream beds, where males bask with wings open and can be territorial. Quite wary; if disturbed flies away strongly and may rest hidden on a tree trunk with wings closed before returning to original perch. Active by day and adults feed on tree sap and overripe fruits, rarely at flowers. Caterpillars feed on Chinese Greenbrier *Smilax china* and other *Smilax* species in greenbrier (Smilaceae) family. Adults seen year round.

Caterpillar

▪ NYMPHALIDAE ▪

Asian Comma ▪ *Polygonia c-aureum* 黃鉤蛺蝶 WS 45–55mm

DESCRIPTION Medium-sized orange butterfly with ragged wings and black spots above. Complex brown pattern below resembling a dead leaf, often with a distinctive white 'comma' in hindwing-centre. Sexes similar. **DISTRIBUTION** Rare overall. Not seen in HKI or Lantau; rare in NT. Otherwise found from India to central and northern China, Korea, and Japan, through mainland SE Asia, to Borneo and the Philippines. **HABITAT AND HABITS** Occurs in wooded areas, but can range widely. Active by day and rests with wings open or closed. Males can be territorial and adults sip nectar. Caterpillars feed on Japanese Hops *Humulus scandens* in hackberry (Cannabaceae) family. Adults seen in any month of the year.

Painted Lady ▪ *Vanessa cardui* 小紅蛺蝶 WS 55mm

DESCRIPTION Medium-sized butterfly. Black, orange and brown above, including orange in hindwing-centre. Below hindwing has dead-leaf pattern with clear eye-spots. Sexes similar. **DISTRIBUTION** Uncommon. Rare in HKI and Lantau; uncommon in NT. Otherwise nearly global in distribution, except for Australasia, South America and Antarctica. **HABITAT AND HABITS** Occurs in open areas, and rests with wings open or closed. Well-known migrant, with swift flight. Active by day and male usually found hilltopping. Adults sip nectar. Caterpillars not known from HK, but elsewhere feed on roughly 300 different host plants, mainly in sunflower (Asteraceae) family. Migrant adults from north seen Aug–May, mainly in autumn. Numbers vary from year to year.

◼ NYMPHALIDAE ◼

Indian Red Admiral ◼ *Vanessa indica* 大紅蛺蝶 WS 60mm

DESCRIPTION Medium-sized butterfly. Black, orange and brown above, lacking orange in middle of hindwing. Below hindwing has dead-leaf pattern without clear eye-spots. Sexes similar. **DISTRIBUTION** Uncommon in HKI and Lantau; fairly common in NT. Otherwise found from Afghanistan to southeastern Russia and Japan, through mainland SE Asia and the Philippines. **HABITAT AND HABITS** Occurs in open areas, and rests with wings open or closed. Known to migrate, and flight swift. Males hilltop territorially and females usually found near villages. Active by day and adults sip nectar. Caterpillars feed on Dense-flowered False Nettle *Boehmeria densiflora* and Ramie False Nettle *B. nivea* in nettle (Urticaceae) family. Adults seen year round.

Common Jester ◼ *Symbrenthia lilaea* 散紋盛蛺蝶 WS 60–65mm

DESCRIPTION Medium-sized black butterfly with three horizontal and one diagonal orange stripes above. Small orange spot above at wing apex, and striking fawn-brown below with irregular brown markings. Most similar to female Colour Sergeant and Orange Staff Sergeant (pp. 103 and 104), but has short wing-tail and lacks their stripes below. Sexes similar. **DISTRIBUTION** Common in HKI, NT and Lantau. Otherwise found from India to central and southern China, through SE Asia, to Borneo and the Philippines. **HABITAT AND HABITS** Occurs in wooded areas and along trails. Can be territorial from a perch, chasing away rivals in moderately strong flight. Active by day; wings held flat or closed at rest. Adults feed on nectar and males congregate to puddle. Unusual in that many eggs are laid together, not just a single egg as in most butterflies. Caterpillars feed on Dense-flowered False Nettle *Boehmeria densiflora* and Ramie False Nettle *B. nivea* in nettle (Urticaceae) family. Adults seen year round.

NYMPHALIDAE

Danaid Eggfly
Hypolimnas misippus 金斑蛺蝶 WS 60–80mm

DESCRIPTION Medium-sized butterfly. Male similar to Great Eggfly (p. 122) above but lacks blue gloss, with larger white patches. Male reddish-brown below with large white patches and black and white trailing margin. Female mimics toxic Plain Tiger Butterfly (p. 72). Best distinguished by extra white apical spot above and below, clearer black hindwing-veins, and serrated hindwing-margin. **DISTRIBUTION** Uncommon in HKI and Lantau; fairly common in NT. Otherwise found from Caribbean Sea, Sub-Saharan Africa, through Indian Ocean to India, to southern China through SE Asia, to Australia as far as Fiji. **HABITAT AND HABITS** Males most often seen hilltopping; less common females occur in open, agricultural areas. Male flight strong and female imitates slow flight of Plain Tiger unless disturbed, when flight rapid. Active by day, and rests with wings open or closed. Known to migrate and capable of travelling long distances, including thousands of kilometres over Atlantic Ocean. Adults sip nectar. Caterpillars rarely, if ever, found in HK. Elsewhere a wide variety of host plants is used, including Morning Glory *Ipomoea* plants in morning glory (Convolvulaceae) family. Adults seen in any month.

Male

Male

Female

Female

NYMPHALIDAE

Great Eggfly ■ *Hypolimnas bolina* 幻紫斑蛺蝶 WS 65–100mm

DESCRIPTION Medium to large butterfly. Mimics toxic Blue-spotted Crow Butterfly (p. 78): male black above with white patches and blue gloss. Female black above with white marginal spotting. Below, both sexes dark brown with white marginal spotting and white band each on forewing and hindwing. Female can have a variety of patterns due to complex genetic variation, including alternate, male-like form with added orange patch above. **DISTRIBUTION** Common in HKI, NT and Lantau. Otherwise found from India to southern China, through SE Asia, to Australia, New Zealand and South Pacific islands east to Marquesas. In the west, also an outpost in Madagascar. **HABITAT AND HABITS** Occurs in wooded and relatively open areas, where both sexes can be territorial. Male flight fairly strong; female imitates slow flight of Blue-spotted Crow. Active by day and rests with wings open or closed. Known to migrate, and males sometimes hilltop. Adults sip nectar. Caterpillars feed on Ivy-like Merremia *Merremia hederacea*, Sweet Potato *Ipomoea batatas* and Three-lobed Morning Glory *I. triloba* in morning glory (Convolvulaceae) family, plus Alligatorweed *Alternanthera philoxeroides* in amaranth (Amaranthaceae) family. Adults seen year round, female more commonly than male.

Male

Female

Female

Female, alternative form

▪ NYMPHALIDAE ▪

Blue Pansy ▪ *Junonia orithya* 翠藍眼蛺蝶 WS 50mm

Male

DESCRIPTION Medium-sized butterfly. Black above with cream diagonal bands and vivid blue on hindwing, less so in female. Reddish hindwing eye-spots, and brown below without clear pattern. Hindwing-margin more rounded than in Peacock and Chocolate Pansies (pp. 125 and 126). **DISTRIBUTION** Uncommon in HKI, NT and Lantau. Otherwise found from Africa and the Middle East, to India and southern China, through SE Asia, to Indonesia, the Philippines and Australia. **HABITAT AND HABITS** Occurs in dry grassland. Flight rapid. Rests on roads with wings open, especially when basking. Active by day and adults sip nectar. Caterpillars feed on Purple Justicia *Justicia procumbens* in acanthus (Acanthaceae) family, Witchweed *Striga asiatica* (*lutea*) in broomrape (Orobanchaceae) family, and Snapdragon *Antirrhinum majus* in figwort (Scrophulariaceae) family. Adults seen year round.

Male   *Female*

123

◾ NYMPHALIDAE ◾

Lemon Pansy ◾ *Junonia lemonias* 蛇眼蛺蝶 WS 60–65mm

DESCRIPTION Medium-sized butterfly. Brown above with yellow flecks and distinct orange eye-spots. Lighter below, rarely with pink suffusion, and additional orange eye-spots. Sexes similar. **DISTRIBUTION** Common in HKI, NT and Lantau. Otherwise found from India to southern China, through SE Asia, to Borneo and the Philippines. **HABITAT AND HABITS** Occurs in open areas at low levels, including in abandoned fields. Flight fairly strong. Active by day and rests with wings open, especially when basking. Adults sip nectar. Caterpillars feed on Curved Lepidagathis *Lepidagathis incurva*, Philippine Violet *Barleria cristata* and Blue Eranthemum *Eranthemum pulchellum* in acanthus (Acanthaceae) family. Adults seen year round.

Unusual 'pink' form

Grey Pansy ◾ *Junonia atlites* 波紋眼蛺蝶 WS 60–65mm

DESCRIPTION Medium-sized butterfly. Brownish-grey with orange eye-spots above and below. Lighter below, and sexes similar. **DISTRIBUTION** Uncommon in HKI and NT; fairly common in Lantau. Otherwise found from India to southern China, through SE Asia, to Indonesia and the Philippines. **HABITAT AND HABITS** Occurs near freshwater wetlands. Flight fairly slow. Rests on the ground with wings open, especially when basking. Active by day and adults sip nectar. Caterpillars feed on Large-flowered Swampweed *Hygrophila ringens* (*lancea*, *salicifolia*) in acanthus (Acanthaceae) family, Procumbent False Pimpernel *Lindernia procumbens* in lindernia (Linderniaceae) family and Alligatorweed *Alternanthera philoxeroides* in amaranth (Amaranthaceae) family. Adults seen year round.

NYMPHALIDAE

Peacock Pansy
Junonia almana 美眼蛺蝶 WS 60–65mm

DESCRIPTION
Medium-sized butterfly. Orange above and tawny below with conspicuous eye-spots in wet-season form. Dry-season form similar above but brown below without eye-spots, similar to Chocolate Pansy (p. 126) below. Peacock Pansy often separable by close inspection of forewing-apex underside, which is darkest at trailing edge and top edge has slight indentation (v lighter at trailing edge and flat on top in Chocolate). Sexes similar.

Wet-season form

DISTRIBUTION Uncommon. Not seen in HKI; uncommon in NT and Lantau. Otherwise found from India to central China and Japan, through SE Asia, to Borneo and the Philippines. **HABITAT AND HABITS** Occurs in grassy areas and abandoned agricultural fields. Flight fairly slow. Active by day and rests on the ground with wings open, especially when basking. Adults sip nectar. Caterpillars feed on Large-flowered Swampweed *Hygrophila ringens* (*lancea*) in acanthus (Acanthaceae) family and Alligatorweed *Alternanthera philoxeroides* in amaranth (Amaranthaceae) family. Adults seen year round.

Wet-season form

Dry-season form

■ Nymphalidae/ Riodinidae ■

Chocolate Pansy ■ *Junonia iphita* 鉤翅眼蛺蝶 WS 60–65mm

DESCRIPTION Medium-sized butterfly. Brown above and below, without notable eye-spots and with leaf-like, curved wing shape. Some individuals have white underside-spot (form *siccata*). See Peacock Pansy (p. 125) for additional notes. Sexes similar. **DISTRIBUTION** Common in HKI, NT and Lantau. Otherwise found from India to southern China, through SE Asia, to Borneo and the Philippines. **HABITAT AND HABITS** Occurs in wooded and semi-open areas. Flight fairly slow. Active by day and rests near the ground with wings open, especially when basking. Adults sip nectar. Caterpillar food plants not well understood in HK, but elsewhere known to feed on several plants in acanthus (Acanthaceae) family. Adults seen year round.

siccata

Punchinello ■ *Zemeros flegyas* 波蜆蝶 WS 35–40mm

DESCRIPTION Small metalmark. Reddish-brown above and below with distinctive pattern of white dots. Sexes similar. **DISTRIBUTION** Common in HKI, NT and Lantau. Otherwise found from India to southern China, through SE Asia, to Borneo and the Philippines. **HABITAT AND HABITS** Occurs in shrubland, sometimes guarding a path-side territory. Active by day. Skips from leaf to leaf, and swivels backwards and forwards on leaf surface with wings half open. At dusk can be seen chasing each other along forest paths. Adults sip nectar. Caterpillars feed on Japanese Maesa *Maesa japonica* and *M. perlaria* in primrose (Primulaceae) family. Adults seen year round.

▪ RIODINIDAE ▪

Plum Judy ▪ *Abisara echerius* 蛇目褐蜆蝶 WS 35–40mm

DESCRIPTION Small metalmark. Dark reddish-brown above and below with black marginal hindwing-spots. Dry-season form duller than wet-season form. Sexes similar.
DISTRIBUTION Common in HKI, NT and Lantau. Otherwise found from India to southern China, through SE Asia, to Borneo, Sulawesi and the Philippines. **HABITAT AND HABITS** Occurs in shrubland and grassland, sometimes guarding a path-side territory. Active by day. Skips from leaf to leaf, and swivels backwards and forwards on leaf surface with wings half open. At dusk can be seen chasing each other along forest paths. Adults sip nectar. Caterpillars feed on Twin-hanging Embelia *Embelia laeta* in primrose (Primulaceae) family. Adults seen year round.

Dry-season form    *Wet-season form*

Orange Punch ▪ *Dodona egeon* 大斑尾蜆蝶 WS 50mm

DESCRIPTION Medium-sized metalmark. Brown and orange above with black stripes. Cream below with black stripes and one wing-tail. Female paler than male.
DISTRIBUTION Uncommon in HKI and NT; rare in Lantau. Otherwise found from India to southern China, through mainland SE Asia. **HABITAT AND HABITS** Occurs in wooded and shrubby areas. Active by day. Flight fairly strong, and males hilltop. Adults sip nectar. Caterpillar host plants not well known, but outside HK other *Dodona* species feed on plants in primrose (Primulaceae) family. Adults seen year round, especially in May.

Female    *Male*

■ LYCAENIDAE ■

Angled Sunbeam ■ *Curetis acuta (dentata)* 尖翅銀灰蝶 WS 40–45mm

Female

DESCRIPTION Medium-sized, blue-like butterfly. Bright white below. Male orange above with broad black margins. Female similar, but with white markings instead of orange.
DISTRIBUTION Uncommon in HKI and NT; not seen in Lantau. Otherwise found from India to central and southern China, through mainland SE Asia. **HABITAT AND HABITS** Occurs in woodland. Active by day. Flight swift, often near canopy, and wings closed at rest except when basking. Adults sip nectar and males mudpuddle. Caterpillars feed on Evergreen Wisteria *Wisteriopsis* (*Callerya*, *Millettia*) *reticulata* and Indian Beech Tree *Pongamia* (*Millettia*) *pinnata* in legume (Fabaceae) family. Adults seen year round.

Male

LYCAENIDAE

Forest Pierrot ■ *Taraka hamada* 蚜灰蝶 WS 20–25mm

DESCRIPTION Small, blue-like butterfly. Dark brown above and white below, with many black spots. Sexes similar. **DISTRIBUTION** Uncommon. Rare in HKI; fairly common in NT; not seen in Lantau. Otherwise found from India to central and southern China, Korea and Japan, through mainland SE Asia, to Borneo. **HABITAT AND HABITS** Occurs in wooded areas, especially around bamboo. Active by day. Flight slow, in undergrowth, and wings closed at rest. Adults do not sip nectar, mainly mudpuddling and rarely found on animal dung. This species and Common Brownie (below) have the only carnivorous caterpillars in HK, feeding on insects rather than plants. Main prey appears to be *Astegopteryx bambusae* aphids in aphid (Aphididae) family, both honeydew secreted by aphids and the insects themselves. The aphids mainly feed on *Bambusa* plants in grass (Poaceae) family. Adults seen year round.

Common Brownie ■ *Miletus chinensis* 中華雲灰蝶 WS 30mm

DESCRIPTION Small, blue-like butterfly. Dark brown above and light grey below, with vague grey patterning. Sexes similar. **DISTRIBUTION** Rare. Not seen in HKI and Lantau; rare in NT. Otherwise found from India to southern China, through mainland SE Asia. **HABITAT AND HABITS** Occurs in wooded and shrubby areas. Active by day, becoming more active at dusk. Flight slow, and wings closed at rest. Adults sip nectar. This species and Forest Pierrot (above) are the only carnivorous caterpillars in HK, feeding on insects rather than plants. Main food sources are Spiraea Aphid *Aphis spiraecola* (*citricola*) in aphid (Aphididae) family, which feeds on Mile-a-Minute Vine *Mikania micrantha* in sunflower (Asteraceae) family, and *Toxoptera odinae* aphids in aphid (Aphididae) family, which feed on *Rhus hypoleuca* in cashew (Anacardiaceae) family. Adults seen year round.

LYCAENIDAE

Long-banded Silverline ▪ *Cigaritis (Spindasis) lohita* 銀線灰蝶
WS 30–35mm

Male

Female

DESCRIPTION Small, blue-like butterfly. Purplish-blue (male) or dark grey (female) above. Light yellow below with reddish (male) or black (female) stripes with silver centres. Lowest basal band long and not broken into three spots, unlike in Club Silverline (opposite). Tornal lobe bright orange; female has less marginal orange on hindwing-upperside than Club, and two thin tails. **DISTRIBUTION** Uncommon in HKI and Lantau; fairly common in NT. Otherwise found from India to southern China, through mainland SE Asia, to Borneo. **HABITAT AND HABITS** Occurs in wooded and shrubby areas. Active by day. Often found resting on plants with wings closed, flying rapidly when disturbed. Adults sip nectar. Caterpillar host plants not well understood in HK, but elsewhere known to feed on a variety of dicot plants, including Turn-in-the-Wind *Mallotus paniculatus* in spurge (Euphorbiaceae) family in Taiwan. Caterpillars thought to be dependent on ants, perhaps including acrobat ant *Crematogaster rogenhoferi*; recent studies have shown that a variety of Long-banded Silverline caterpillar calls prompt these ants to guard the caterpillar. Unlike most other ant-associated caterpillars in gossamer-winged butterfly family, this species not known to reward the ants with sweet secretions. Remarkably, even the pupa emits calls that trigger ant assistance. The mechanism by which caterpillars make these sounds remains unknown. Adults seen Apr–Nov.

= LYCAENIDAE =

Club Silverline = *Cigaritis (Spindasis) syama* 豆粒銀線灰蝶 WS 30mm

DESCRIPTION Small, blue-like butterfly. Purplish-blue (male) or dark grey (female) above. Light yellow below with blackish stripes with silver centres. Lowest basal band broken into three spots, unlike in Long-banded Silverline (opposite). Tornal lobe bright orange. Female has more extensive marginal orange on hindwing-upperside than Long-banded, and two thin tails. **DISTRIBUTION** Uncommon. Not seen in HKI; uncommon in NT and Lantau. Otherwise found from India to southern and central China, through mainland SE Asia, to Borneo and the Philippines. **HABITAT AND HABITS** Occurs in wooded and shrubby areas. Active by day. Often found resting on plants with wings closed, flying rapidly when disturbed. Adults sip nectar. Caterpillars feed on variety of plants, including Mayflower Glorybower *Clerodendrum cyrtophyllum* in mint (Lamiaceae) family. Caterpillars attended by ants, potentially by other *Crematogaster* acrobat ant species than Long-banded. See Long-banded for additional notes on this behaviour. Adults seen Apr–Nov.

Purple Sapphire = *Heliophorus epicles* 彩灰蝶 WS 30mm

DESCRIPTION Small, blue-like butterfly. Distinctive – black and red above, with purple in male. Bright yellow below with orange margins, and one wing-tail. **DISTRIBUTION** Common. Uncommon in HKI; common in NT and Lantau. Otherwise found from India to southern China, through mainland SE Asia. **HABITAT AND HABITS** Occurs in open, shrubby areas. Active by day. Flight fairly strong and low to the ground. Adults sip nectar and hold wings closed at rest, except when basking. Caterpillars feed on Chinese Knotweed *Persicaria* (*Polygonia*) *chinensis* in knotweed (Polygonaceae) family. Adults seen year round.

LYCAENIDAE

Tailless Line Blue ■ *Prosotas dubiosa* 疑波灰蝶 WS 20mm

DESCRIPTION Small blue. Male bluish above and female dark brown with blue at base. Greyish-brown below with multiple white and brown bands, one large, orange-crowned black eye-spot and no wing-tail. **DISTRIBUTION** Fairly common in HKI, NT and Lantau. Otherwise found from India to southern China, through SE Asia, to eastern Indonesia and Australia. **HABITAT AND HABITS** Occurs in forested areas and gardens. Active by day. Brisk, erratic flight, and wings held closed at rest. Adults sip nectar and males often mudpuddle. Caterpillar host plants not well understood in HK, but elsewhere known to feed on a variety of plants in legume (Fabaceae) family, including Ear-leaved Acacia *Acacia auriculiformis*. Adults seen year round.

Common Line Blue ■ *Prosotas nora* 娜拉波灰蝶 WS 20–25mm

DESCRIPTION Small blue. Male bluish-purple above with thin black border; female dark brown with triangle of light blue on forewing. Yellowish-brown below with multiple white and brown bands, one large, orange-crowned black eye-spot and white-tipped, thread-like tail. Female greyer below than male. **DISTRIBUTION** Recent addition to HK; regular since 2018 or so. Now uncommon in HKI and NT; rare in Lantau. Otherwise found from India to southern China, through SE Asia, to eastern Indonesia and the Philippines. **HABITAT AND HABITS** Occurs in forested areas and gardens. Active by day. Brisk, erratic flight, and wings held closed at rest. Adults sip nectar and males often mudpuddle. Caterpillar host plants not well understood in HK, but elsewhere known to feed on variety of plants in legume (Fabaceae) family, including Ear-leaved Acacia *Acacia auriculiformis*. Adults seen Apr–Jan.

▪ LYCAENIDAE ▪

Transparent Six-line Blue ▪ *Nacaduba kurava* 古樓娜灰蝶 WS 30mm

DESCRIPTION Small blue. Male dull pale violet above; female light metallic blue with black margins. Greyish-brown below with pattern of white arcs and one main eye-spot at tornus, plus thin tail. Usually seen from below, and female distinguished from male by greater contrast (especially in wet-season form), with marginal markings darker than those more basal. Determining the sex can be important, because from below female generally considered indistinguishable from Rounded Six-line Blue (p. 134). Transparent tends to be lighter and with straight forewing termen. Termen more rounded in Rounded, with forewing- and hindwing-margins together forming more of 'B' shape. This can be very subtle. Both *Nacaduba* species separable from three *Jamides* species by three (rather than two) forewing-bands of white arcs. **DISTRIBUTION** Fairly common in HKI, NT and Lantau. Otherwise found from India to southern China, through SE Asia, to eastern Indonesia and Australia. **HABITAT AND HABITS** Occurs in wooded areas. Active by day. Fairly strong flight. Males can be territorial, and hilltop. Adults sip nectar and hold wings closed at rest. Caterpillar diet not well understood in HK; probably *Maesa* plants in primrose (Primulaceae) family. Elsewhere reported to feed on *Ardisia* and *Embelia* plants, also in primrose (Primulacaeae) family. Adults seen year round.

Male

Female

▪ LYCAENIDAE ▪

Rounded Six-line Blue ▪ *Nacaduba berenice* 百娜灰蝶 WS 25–30mm

DESCRIPTION Small blue. Male greyish-blue above and female greyish-blue with broad black margins, significantly darker on hindwing than in Transparent Six-line Blue (p. 133). Greyish-brown below with pattern of white arcs and one main tornal eye-spot, plus thin tail. See Transparent for more detail, but often unidentifiable to species level in the field. Both *Nacaduba* species distinguishable from three *Jamides* species by three (rather than two) forewing-bands of white arcs. **DISTRIBUTION** Overlooked in HK for many years, now uncommonly identified. Rare in HK; uncommon in NT and Lantau. Otherwise found from India to southern China, through SE Asia, to eastern Indonesia and Australia. **HABITAT AND HABITS** Occurs in wooded areas. Active by day. Fairly strong flight. Males can be territorial, and hilltop. Adults sip nectar and hold wings closed at rest. Caterpillars feed on Lychee *Litchi chinensis* in soapberry (Sapindaceae) family. Adults seen year round except Feb.

Male    *Male*

Common Cerulean ▪ *Jamides celeno* 錫冷雅灰蝶 WS 30–35mm

DESCRIPTION Small blue. Male and female pale blue above, with relatively thin black margins. Brown below with two forewing-bands of white arcs, one large, orange-crowned black eye-spot and thin tail. Less brown below than Dark Cerulean (opposite), and upper white arcs in straight row, unlike in Metallic Cerulean (opposite). Also, unlike these two species, Common has two white forewing costal spots. **DISTRIBUTION** Uncommon. Rare in HKI; uncommon in NT and Lantau. Otherwise found from India to southern China, through mainland SE Asia, to Indonesia and the Philippines. **HABITAT AND HABITS** Occurs in secondary growth and gardens. Active by day. Slow, erratic flight, and wings held closed at rest. Adults sip nectar. Caterpillar host plants not well understood in HK, but thought to include Indian Beech Tree *Pongamia* (*Millettia*) *pinnata* and Common Derris *Derris trifoliata* in legume (Fabaceae) family. Adults seen year round, especially Nov.

▪ LYCAENIDAE ▪

Dark Cerulean ▪ *Jamides bochus* 雅灰蝶 WS 25–30mm

DESCRIPTION Small blue. Male deep metallic blue above and female paler blue; both with wide black margins. Brown below with two forewing-bands of white arcs, one large, orange-crowned black eye-spot and thin tail. Smallest local *Jamides*, and plainest brown below. Lacks two white forewing costal spots of Common Cerulean (opposite). **DISTRIBUTION** Fairly common in HKI, NT and Lantau. Otherwise found from India, to southern and central China, through mainland SE Asia, to Borneo and the Philippines. **HABITAT AND HABITS** Occurs in woodland and secondary growth. Active by day. Brisk, erratic flight, and wings held closed at rest. Adults sip nectar. Caterpillars feed on buds of Tropical Kudzu *Neustanthus* (*Pueraria*) *phaseoloides*, Montane Kudzu *Pueraria montana* (*lobata*) and Glittering-leaved Callerya *Callerya* (*Millettia*) *nitida* in legume (Fabaceae) family. Adults seen May–Dec.

Metallic Cerulean ▪ *Jamides alecto* 素雅灰蝶 WS 35–40mm

DESCRIPTION Small blue. Male and female light blue above, with black margins. Brown below with two forewing-bands of white arcs, one large, orange-crowned black eye-spot and thin tail. The largest cerulean, with brighter white markings below than Dark Cerulean (above), and upper white arcs not in straight row as in Common Cerulean (opposite). Also lacks two white forewing costal spots of Common. **DISTRIBUTION** Fairly common in HKI, NT and Lantau. Otherwise found from India to southern China, through mainland SE Asia, to Borneo and the Philippines. **HABITAT AND HABITS** Occurs in secondary growth and gardens. Active by day. Brisk, erratic flight, and wings held closed at rest. Adults sip nectar. Caterpillar host plants not well understood in HK, but elsewhere known to feed on plants in ginger (Zingiberaceae) family. Adults seen year round.

◾ LYCAENIDAE ◾

Pea Blue ◾ *Lampides boeticus* 亮灰蝶 WS 30–35mm

Male

DESCRIPTION
Small blue. Above light purple (male) or greyish-blue with dark margins (female) and two black eye-spots. Below brownish with white pattern, including distinctive white submarginal band, two orange-crowned black eye-spots and one wing-tail. **DISTRIBUTION** Common in HKI, NT and Lantau. Otherwise found widely in the Old World, from Azores and Europe, through Africa, the Middle East, South Asia, to Japan and SE Asia, to Australia and New Zealand, and Tahiti and Hawaii. **HABITAT AND HABITS** Occurs in shrubland and weedy areas. Known to migrate, and active by day. Flight strong and wings held closed at rest. Adults sip nectar and males hilltop. Caterpillars feed on flowers (not leaves) of Streaked Rattlepod *Crotalaria pallida*, Rattleweed *C. retusa*, Cowpea *Vigna unguiculata*, Glittering-leaved Callerya *Callerya* (*Millettia*) *nitida*, Montane Kudzu *Pueraria montana* (*lobata*) and Thunberg's Lespedeza *Lespedeza thunbergii* (*formosa*) in legume (Fabaceae) family, Adults seen year round.

Male    *Female*

LYCAENIDAE

Forget-Me-Not ■ *Catochrysops strabo* 咖灰蝶 WS 25–30mm

DESCRIPTION Small blue. Above light purple with one marginal eye-spot (male), or blue with dark margins and multiple marginal eye-spots (female). Below greyish-brown, with medium brown arcs, one large eye-spot (with large amount of orange) and one wing-tail. Small but distinct forewing-underside costal spot, centred between two brown arcs. **DISTRIBUTION** Fairly common in HKI, NT and Lantau. Otherwise found from India to southern China, through SE Asia, to Indonesia and the Philippines. **HABITAT AND HABITS** Occurs in shrubby secondary growth. Active by day; wings held closed at rest. Flight rapid and adults sip nectar. Caterpillars feed on flowers (not leaves) of Hairy Phyllodium *Phyllodium elegans*, Rosary Pea *Abrus precatorius*, *Dunbaria punctata* (*rotundifolia*) and Asian Ticktrefoil *Grona* (*Desmodium*) *heterocarpos* in Legume (Fabaceae) family. Adults seen year round.

Male

Male

Female

Silver Forget-Me-Not ■ *Catochrysops panormus* 藍咖灰蝶 WS 30–35mm

DESCRIPTION Small blue. Above light blue with one marginal eye-spot (male) or blue with dark margins and multiple marginal eye-spots (female). Below grey, with brownish-grey arcs, one large eye-spot (with less orange than in Forget-Me-Not, above), and one wing-tail. Lacks distinct forewing-underside costal spot of Forget-Me-Not. If present it is smaller and closer to costa; not centred but closer to second arc. **DISTRIBUTION** Rare. Not seen in HKI and NT; rare in Lantau. Otherwise found from India to southern China, through SE Asia, to Indonesia, the Philippines, Australia and New Caledonia. **HABITAT AND HABITS** Occurs in weedy areas and secondary growth. Active by day; wings held closed at rest. Flight erratic and rapid. Adults sip nectar and males mudpuddle. Caterpillar host plants not well understood in HK, but elsewhere feeds on Tropical Kudzu *Neustanthus* (*Pueraria*) *phaseoloides* and *Dendrolobium* in legume (Fabaceae) family. Adults only seen Oct.

Male

▪ LYCAENIDAE ▪

Gram Blue ▪ *Euchrysops cnejus* 棕灰蝶 WS 25–30mm

DESCRIPTION Small blue. Above light purple with two marginal eye-spots (male) or grey with blue in forewing-centre and multiple marginal eye-spots (female). Below grey, with black and tan markings, and one wing-tail placed between two large eye-spots.
DISTRIBUTION Uncommon in HKI, NT and Lantau. Otherwise found from India to southern China, through SE Asia to Indonesia, the Philippines and Australia, east to Tonga. **HABITAT AND HABITS** Occurs in gardens, agricultural areas and secondary growth. Active by day and wings held closed at rest. Flight erratic and rapid, near the ground. Adults sip nectar. Caterpillars may be attended by ants and feed on flowers (not leaves) of Rosary Pea *Abrus precatorius*, Black Gram (Urad Dal) *Vigna mungo*, *V. minima*, Beach Bean *Canavalia rosea* (*maritima*) and Tropical Kudzu *Neustanthus* (*Pueraria*) *phaseoloides* in legume (Fabaceae) family. Adults seen Feb–Nov.

Male  *Female*

Orange-tipped Pea-Blue ▪ *Everes lacturnus* 長尾藍灰蝶 WS 25mm

DESCRIPTION Small blue. Above purple with black margins (male) or light blue with thick black margins and multiple marginal eye-spots (female). Below greyish-white, with black and grey markings, and one wing-tail placed below two large eye-spots.
DISTRIBUTION Uncommon in HKI, NT and Lantau. Otherwise found from India to southern China, through SE Asia, to Indonesia, the Philippines and Australia. **HABITAT AND HABITS** Occurs in weedy areas and shrubland. Active by day and wings held closed at rest. Flight weak and low. Adults sip nectar. Caterpillars feed on seedpods (not leaves) of Asian Ticktrefoil *Grona* (*Desmodium*) *heterocarpos* and *G.* (*Desmodium*) *reticulata* in legume (Fabaceae) family. Adults seen Apr–Nov.

LYCAENIDAE

Plains Cupid ■ *Luthrodes (Chilades) pandava* 曲紋紫灰蝶 WS 30mm

Male

DESCRIPTION Small blue. Above purple with black margins (male) or dark grey with blue wing centres with thick black margins, and multiple marginal eye-spots (female). Below greyish-brown with white arcs, black spots and one wing-tail placed below one large eye-spot and above two smaller eye-spots. **DISTRIBUTION** Common in HKI and NT; uncommon in Lantau. Otherwise found from India and islands in Indian Ocean, to central China and Japan, through SE Asia, to Borneo and the Philippines. **HABITAT AND HABITS** Seen in parks near host plant. Active by day; wings held closed at rest. Flight moderate. Adults sip nectar. Uniquely among HK butterflies, caterpillars do not feed on an Angiospermae flowering plant. Instead, food plant is Sago Cycad *Sago revoluta*, a non-native member of the ancient group of cycad plants, class Cycadopsida. May be attended by ants. Adults seen Apr–Dec. One of the few HK butterflies that is not native, having spread by introduction of its host plants for landscaping.

Male

Female

■ LYCAENIDAE ■

Jewelled Grass Blue ■ *Freyeria (Chilades) putli* 普紫灰蝶 WS 20mm

DESCRIPTION Small blue. Above dark brown with black marginal hindwing-spots. Below brown with brown and white spotting and four black eye-spots with orange edges. No wing-tail. Sexes similar. **DISTRIBUTION** Uncommon in HKI and Lantau; rare in NT. Otherwise found from India to southern China, through mainland SE Asia, to Indonesia and Australia. **HABITAT AND HABITS** Seen in open grassy areas and scrubland. Active by day; wings held closed at rest. Flight slow and near the ground. Adults sip nectar. Caterpillar food plants not well understood in HK, but thought to feed on Hairy Indigo *Indigofera hirsuta* in legume (Fabaceae) family. Adults only seen Sep–early Nov.

Zebra Blue ■ *Leptotes (Syntarucus) plinius* 細灰蝶 WS 25–30mm

DESCRIPTION Small blue. Above male dull violet-blue; female blue with thick black margin, marginal hindwing-spots and distinctive black forewing-spots. Underside pattern unique for a blue, with dark splotches, two tornal eye-spots and one wing-tail. **DISTRIBUTION** Rare in HKI and NT; not seen in Lantau. Otherwise found from India to southern China, through mainland SE Asia, to Indonesia and Australia. **HABITAT AND HABITS** Occurs in open, shrubby and wooded areas. Active by day. Flight slow and low to the ground. Adults sip nectar and hold wings closed at rest. Caterpillar food plants not well understood in HK, but elsewhere reported to feed on variety of plants in legume (Fabaceae) family. Adults seen in Dec (not every year), occasionally in spring.

LYCAENIDAE

Lime Blue   Chilades lajus 紫灰蝶 WS 25–30mm

DESCRIPTION Small blue. Above dark purple with black margins (male) or dark grey with purple wing-centres with thick black margins and black spots (female). Below grey with fairly large, dark markings, paler and fainter in dry-season form. No wing-tail. **DISTRIBUTION** Fairly common in HKI; uncommon in NT; common in Lantau. Otherwise found from India to southern China, through SE Asia. **HABITAT AND HABITS** Seen in open areas and shrubby secondary growth, often near coast. Active by day; wings held closed at rest. Flight slow and near the ground. Adults sip nectar. Attended by Nicobar Carpenter Ants *Camponotus nicobarensis*, and caterpillars feed on Chinese Box-Orange *Severinia* (*Atalantia*) *buxifolia* in citrus (Rutaceae) family. Adults seen year round.

Wet-season form

Dry-season form

Male

▪ LYCAENIDAE ▪

Common Hedge Blue ▪ *Acytolepis puspa* 鈕灰蝶 WS 30mm

Male

Male

DESCRIPTION Small blue. Male purplish-blue above with black margins and whitish wing-centres; female light blue and white above with wide black margins. White below with black spots, greyer in female. Male Plain Hedge Blue (opposite) has narrower black margin above on forewing termen and lacks whitish wing-centres. From below, male Common ground colour whiter, with blacker spots and one extra (small) basal hindwing-spot. In both species, submarginal row has 'skewed' mark not in line. No wing-tail. **DISTRIBUTION** Common in HKI, NT and Lantau. Otherwise found from India to southern China, through SE Asia, to Borneo and the Philippines. **HABITAT AND HABITS** Occurs in shrubby areas and secondary growth. Active by day. Flight of medium speed; wings held closed at rest. Adults sip nectar and mudpuddle, and males hilltop. Caterpillars may be attended by Rich Spiny Sugar Ants *Polyrhachis dives* and feed on wide variety of plants, including Glittering-leaved Callerya *Callerya* (*Millettia*) *nitida*, Scarlet Powder-Puff *Calliandra haematocephala*, Orchid Tree *Bauhinia purpurea* and Yellow Flame Tree *Peltophorum pterocarpum* in legume (Fabaceae) family, as well as Pop-gun Seed *Bridelia tomentosa* and *B. insulana* (Euphorbiaceae), Hiptage *Hiptage benghalensis* (Malphigiaceae), Lychee *Litchi chinensis* (Sapindaceae) and Bentham's Photinia *Photinia benthamiana* (Rosaceae). Adults seen year round.

Female

LYCAENIDAE

Plain Hedge Blue ■ *Celastrina lavendularis* 薰衣琉璃灰蝶 WS 25mm

DESCRIPTION Small blue. Male purplish-blue above with black margins without whitish wing centres; female usually similar. Grey below with mainly dark grey spots (ringed with white), paler in female. No wing-tail. See Common Hedge Blue (opposite) for further details. **DISTRIBUTION** Uncommon in HKI and NT; not seen in Lantau. Otherwise found from India to southern China, through SE Asia, to eastern Indonesia and the Philippines. **HABITAT AND HABITS** Occurs in shrubby areas and secondary growth. Active by day. Flight of medium speed; wings held closed at rest. Adults sip nectar and mudpuddle, and males hilltop. Caterpillar host plants not well understood. Adults seen year round.

Male

Female

143

▪ LYCAENIDAE ▪

Pale Hedge Blue ▪ *Udara dilecta* 嫵灰蝶 WS 25mm

DESCRIPTION Small blue. Male light purplish-blue above with thin black margin and whitish wing centres; female light blue with white wing centres and fairly wide black margin, especially forewing. White below with mostly light grey spots, which is fairly distinctive. Unlike in Common and Plain Hedge Blues (pp. 142 and 143), submarginal row does not have mark that is skewed out of line. Also has backwards 'L'-shaped mark near bottom of hindwing and faint 'outline' of marginal spots, like the letter 'M'. No wing-tail. **DISTRIBUTION** Rare. Not seen in HKI; rare in NT and Lantau. Otherwise found from India, to central and southern China, through SE Asia, to eastern Indonesia. **HABITAT AND HABITS** Occurs in shrubby areas and secondary growth. Active by day. Flight slow; wings held closed at rest. Adults sip nectar and mudpuddle, and males hilltop. Caterpillar host plants not well understood in HK, but elsewhere known to feed on *Castanopsis* in beech (Fagaceae) family. Adults seen Mar–May.

Albocerulean ▪ *Udara albocaerulea* 白斑嫵灰蝶 WS 30–35mm

DESCRIPTION Small blue. Male light blue above with black forewing apex and whitish wing centres; female similar but greyish-brown instead of blue. Bright white below with few black spots, which are lighter in female. Unlike in Common and Plain Hedge Blues (pp. 142 and 143), submarginal row lacks a mark that is skewed out of line. No outlining of marginal spotting, and no wing-tail. **DISTRIBUTION** Rare. Not seen in HKI and Lantau; uncommon in NT. Otherwise found from India to central and southern China to Japan, through SE Asia, to Indonesia. **HABITAT AND HABITS** Occurs in wooded areas and secondary growth. Active by day. Flight moderate; wings held closed at rest. Adults sip nectar and mudpuddle. Caterpillars feed on flower buds of Sweet Viburnum *Viburnum odoratissimum* in elder (Viburnaceae) family. Adults seen Dec–May.

Male    *Female*

LYCAENIDAE

Malayan ◼ *Megisba malaya* 美姬灰蝶 WS 25–30mm

DESCRIPTION Small blue. Brown above with bluish tinge. White below with distinctive spot pattern. Female plainer below than male. Large hindwing costal spot similar to that of Quaker (below). One short wing-tail. **DISTRIBUTION** Uncommon in HKI and NT; fairly common in Lantau. Otherwise found from India to southern China, through SE Asia, to Borneo. **HABITAT AND HABITS** Occurs in forested areas. Active by day. Flight weak; wings held closed at rest. Adults sip nectar and males mudpuddle. Caterpillar host plants not well understood in HK, but elsewhere known to feed on variety of dicot plants, including Turn-in-the-Wind *Mallotus paniculatus* in spurge (Euphorbiaceae) family. Adults seen Sep–Jan.

Male   Female

Quaker ◼ *Neopithecops zalmora* 一點灰蝶 WS 20–25mm

DESCRIPTION Small blue. Dark brown above, paler in wing centres. Bright white below with grey patterning and one medium-black hindwing costal spot. No wing-tail, and legs black and white. Sexes similar. **DISTRIBUTION** Uncommon. Not seen in HKI; uncommon in NT; fairly common in Lantau. Otherwise found from India to southern China, through SE Asia, to Borneo and the Philippines. **HABITAT AND HABITS** Occurs in forested areas. Active by day. Flight weak and fluttering, often near the ground, showing striking contrast between dark upperside and white underside. Wings held closed at rest. Adults sip nectar and males mudpuddle. Caterpillars feed on Flower Axistree *Glycosmis parviflora* in citrus (Rutaceae) family. Adults seen year round.

LYCAENIDAE

Forest Quaker
Pithecops corvus 黑丸灰蝶 WS 20–25mm

DESCRIPTION Small blue. Dark brown above. Bright white below with orange submarginal band and one large black hindwing costal spot. No wing-tail, and legs white. Sexes similar. **DISTRIBUTION** Uncommon. Not seen in HKI and Lantau; uncommon in NT. Otherwise found from India to southern China, through SE Asia, to Borneo and the Philippines. **HABITAT AND HABITS** Occurs in forested areas. Active by day. Flight weak and fluttering, often near the ground; note striking contrast between dark upperside and white underside. Wings held closed at rest. Adults sip nectar and males mudpuddle. Caterpillar host plants not well understood in HK, but elsewhere known to feed on *Glycosmis* plants in citrus (Rutaceae) family, *Gardenia* plants in coffee (Rubiaceae) family and Ticktrefoil *Desmodium* plants in legume (Fabaceae) family. Adults seen year round.

Black-spotted Grass Blue
Famegana nisa (alsulus) 珈灰蝶 WS 20–25mm

DESCRIPTION Small blue. Above purplish-blue with fairly thick black margins (male) or dull grey (female). Light grey below with pale marginal markings and distinctive black tornal spot, which is rarely missing. No wing-tail. **DISTRIBUTION** Uncommon. Not seen in HKI; uncommon in NT and Lantau. Otherwise found from southern China, through mainland SE Asia, to Australia. **HABITAT AND HABITS** Occurs in shrubland and weedy grassland. Active by day and wings held closed at rest. Flight weak and low. Adults sip nectar. Caterpillars feed on Beautiful Phyllodium *Phyllodium pulchellum*, Hairy Phyllodium *P. elegans* and Large-leaved Flemingia *Flemingia macrophylla* in legume (Fabaceae) family. Adults seen year round, but mainly Oct–Nov.

LYCAENIDAE

Pale Grass Blue ■ *Pseudozizeeria (Zizeeria) maha* 酢漿灰蝶 WS 25–30mm

DESCRIPTION Small blue with variable size and pattern, especially between seasons. Male blue above with black margins. Female dark grey above with blue at base (wet-season form) or light blue with thick black margins and a few dark marginal spots (dry-season form). Grey below with multiple arcs of dark markings, much plainer in dry-season form. In contrast to Dark Grass Blue (p. 148), marginal markings on wing edge not substantially paler than submarginal markings. No wing-tail. **DISTRIBUTION** Common in HKI, NT and Lantau. Otherwise found from India to northern China, Korea and Japan, through SE Asia, to Borneo and the Philippines. **HABITAT AND HABITS** Occurs in parks, weedy areas and shrubland. Active by day; wings held closed at rest. Flight weak and low. Adults sip nectar. Caterpillars feed on Creeping Woodsorrel *Oxalis corniculata* in woodsorrel (Oxalidaceae) family. Adults seen year round.

Wet-season form

Dry-season form

Male

Female, wet-season form

Female, dry-season form

▪ LYCAENIDAE ▪

Dark Grass Blue ▪ *Zizeeria karsandra* 吉灰蝶 WS 20–25mm

Male

Male

DESCRIPTION Small blue similar to Pale Grass Blue (p. 147), but smaller. Male more purplish-blue above with thicker black margins. From below, best identified by marginal markings paler than submarginal markings. On close inspection in the hand, Dark's forewing lacks sub-basal spot in space CuA_2 below. No wing-tail. **DISTRIBUTION** Rare. Uncommon in HKI and NT; rare in Lantau. Otherwise found from the Middle East and India to southern China, through SE Asia, to Borneo and the Philippines, extending to Australia. **HABITAT AND HABITS** Occurs in shrubland and weedy areas. Active by day; wings held closed at rest. Flight weak and low. Adults sip nectar. Caterpillars feed on Green Amaranth *Amaranthus viridis*, Tricolour Amaranth *A. tricolour* and Spiny Amaranth *A. spinosus* in amaranth (Amaranthaceae) family. Adults seen year round.

Female

◾ LYCAENIDAE ◾

Lesser Grass Blue ◾ *Zizina otis* 毛眼灰蝶 WS 20–25mm

DESCRIPTION Small blue similar to Pale Grass Blue (p. 147), but smaller. Male more purplish-blue above, similar to Dark Grass Blue (opposite), but black hindwing-margin does not extend all the way around. Below, Lesser similar to Dark, with marginal markings paler than submarginal markings. However, Lesser lacks forewing costal spot and forewing cell spot, and hindwing Rs space costal spot is shifted inwards, out of line with arc. No wing-tail. **DISTRIBUTION** Fairly common in HKI, NT and Lantau. Otherwise found widely in the Old World, from Sub-Saharan Africa, through India, to southern China, through SE Asia, to Australia and New Zealand, all the way to Tahiti and Hawaii.

HABITAT AND HABITS Occurs in shrubland and weedy areas. Active by day; wings held closed at rest. Flight weak and low. Adults sip nectar. Caterpillars feed on Creeping Tick Trefoil *Grona* (*Desmodium*) *triflora* and *Zornia gibbosa* in legume (Fabaceae) family. Adults seen year round.

Male

Male

Tiny Grass Blue ◾ *Zizula hylax* 長腹灰蝶 WS 15–20mm

DESCRIPTION Tiny blue. Male dull violet-blue above and female brown. Typical pattern of blues below – grey with black and grey dots. Look for inverted 'V'-shaped dot in arc of forewing dots (often the fourth dot, counting from costal margin), and especially two forewing costal margin dots, distinctive for this species. No wing-tail. **DISTRIBUTION** Uncommon in HKI and NT; fairly common in Lantau. Otherwise found widely in the Old World, from Sub-Saharan Africa and the Middle East, through India to southern China, through SE Asia and Australia, all the way to the Cook Islands. **HABITAT AND HABITS** Occurs in open, grassy areas. Active by day. Fluttering flight rapid and erratic, often low to the ground. Adults sip nectar; hold wings closed at rest. Caterpillar food plants not well understood in HK, but elsewhere reported to feed on variety of plants in acanthus (Acanthaceae) family, including Large-flowered Swampweed *Hygrophila ringens* (*lancea*, *salicifolia*). Adults seen year round.

■ LYCAENIDAE ■

Silverstreak Blue ■ *Iraota timoleon* 鐵木萊異灰蝶 WS 40–45mm

DESCRIPTION Medium-sized hairstreak. Black above with metallic blue and one wing-tail (male), or purple with two wing-tails (female). Dark brown below with white blotches. **DISTRIBUTION** Fairly common in HKI and NT; uncommon in Lantau. Otherwise found from India to southern China, through mainland SE Asia to Indonesia. **HABITAT AND HABITS** Occurs in wooded areas and near Longan *Dimocarpus longan* and Lychee *Litchi chinensis* orchards. Active by day. Flight swift and often at canopy level. Males hilltop. Adults feed on nectar and some fruits, and hold wings closed at rest except when basking. Caterpillars feed on Superb Fig *Ficus subpisocarpa* (*superba*) in mulberry and fig (Moraceae) family. Adults seen year round.

Male

Female

Falcate Oakblue ■ *Mahathala ameria* 瑪灰蝶 WS 35–40mm

DESCRIPTION Small hairstreak with distinctive wing shape. Black above with metallic purple patches. Dark brown below with one wing-tail. **DISTRIBUTION** Uncommon. Rare in HKI; uncommon in NT and Lantau. Otherwise found from India to central and southern China, through mainland SE Asia. **HABITAT AND HABITS** Occurs in forested areas. Active by day. Flight swift. Adults feed on nectar; hold wings closed at rest. Caterpillars attended by ants and feed on Climbing Mallotus *Mallotus repandus* in spurge (Euphorbiaceae) family. Adults seen year round.

Caterpillar with Polyrhachis *spiny ant*

■ LYCAENIDAE ■

Powdered Oakblue ■ *Arhopala bazalus* 百嬈灰蝶 WS 45mm

DESCRIPTION Medium-sized hairstreak. Dark brown above, female having metallic purple on forewing. Dark brown below with subtle spots and one wing-tail. **DISTRIBUTION** Uncommon in HKI and NT; not seen in Lantau. Otherwise found from India to central and southern China to Japan, and through mainland SE Asia. **HABITAT AND HABITS** Occurs in wooded areas. Active by day. Flight swift, but spends much time resting inconspicuously in shade. Adults feed on nectar, holding wings closed at rest except when basking. Caterpillars attended by ants. Host plants not well understood in HK, but elsewhere known to feed on Stone Oak *Lithocarpus* plants in beech (Fagaceae) family. Adults seen year round.

Male

Female

Dull Oakblue ■ *Arhopala centaurus (pseudocentaurus)* 銀鏈嬈灰蝶 WS 55mm

DESCRIPTION Largest hairstreak. Metallic purple above with black margins. Dark brown below with distinctive white arcs on forewing cell, and one wing-tail. **DISTRIBUTION** Rare. Not seen in HKI and Lantau; rare in NT. Otherwise found from India to southern China, through mainland SE Asia, to Borneo, the Philippines and Australia. **HABITAT AND HABITS** Occurs in forested areas. Active by day. Flight swift. Adults feed on nectar and hold wings closed at rest. Caterpillars attended by Asian Weaver Ants *Oecophylla smaragdina*. Host plants not well understood in HK, but elsewhere known to feed on Oak *Quercus* plants in beech (Fagaceae) family. Adults seen in almost all months.

▪ Lycaenidae ▪

Hooked Oakblue ▪ *Arhopala paramuta* 小嬈灰蝶 WS 30–35mm

DESCRIPTION Relatively small hairstreak. Purple above with wide black margins. Light to medium brown below with plain markings. Forewing shape distinctive, with curved termen slight hook to apex, and no wing-tail. **DISTRIBUTION** Rare. Not seen in HKI and Lantau; rare in NT. Otherwise found from India to southern China, through mainland SE Asia. **HABITAT AND HABITS** Occurs in forested areas. Active by day. Flight swift. Adults feed on nectar and hold wings closed at rest. Caterpillars attended by *Polyrhachis vigilans* spiny ants and feed on *Castanopsis fissa* in beech (Fagaceae) family. Adults seen July–Dec, especially Dec.

Burmese Bushblue ▪ *Arhopala birmana* 緬甸嬈灰蝶 WS 35mm

DESCRIPTION Relatively small hairstreak. Metallic purple above with black margins (female light blue). Medium brown with many white markings below, and one wing-tail. **DISTRIBUTION** Uncommon. Not seen in HKI and Lantau; fairly common in NT. Otherwise found from India to southern China, through mainland SE Asia. **HABITAT AND HABITS** Occurs in wooded areas. Active by day. Flight swift and males hilltop. Adults feed on nectar and hold wings closed at rest except when basking. Caterpillars attended by ants and feed on Thick-leaved Oak *Quercus* (*Cyclobalanopsis*) *edithiae* in beech (Fagaceae) family. Adults seen May–Jan.

Male

Female

LYCAENIDAE

Common Onyx ■ *Horaga onyx* 斑灰蝶 WS 30mm

DESCRIPTION Small hairstreak. Black above with white and purplish-blue patches. Brown below with white band (not just white patch as usually seen in Violet Onyx, below), one large eye-spot and three wing-tails. Front legs striped black and white, not mainly white as in Violet. Sexes similar. **DISTRIBUTION** Uncommon in HKI and NT; not seen in Lantau. Otherwise found from India to southern China, through mainland SE Asia, to Borneo. **HABITAT AND HABITS** Occurs in wooded areas. Active by day. Flight swift and males hilltop. Adults feed on nectar and hold wings closed at rest. Caterpillar food plants in HK not well understood, but thought to feed on male flowers of Oblong-leaved Litsea *Litsea rotundifolia* in laurel (Lauraceae) family, and reported from Lychee *Litchi chinensis*. Adults seen year round.

Violet Onyx ■ *Horaga albimacula* 白斑灰蝶 WS 20–30mm

DESCRIPTION Small hairstreak. Blackish-brown above with white patches, and usually lacking metallic blue of Common Onyx (above). Brown below with white patch (that does not usually extend like band of Common), one large eye-spot and three wing-tails. Front legs mainly white, not striped black and white as in Common. Sexes similar. **DISTRIBUTION** Rare in HKI and NT; not seen in Lantau. Otherwise found from India to southern China, through mainland SE Asia, to Borneo. **HABITAT AND HABITS** Occurs in wooded areas and clearings. Active by day. Flight weak. Adults feed on nectar and hold wings closed at rest. Caterpillar food plants in HK not well understood, but reported from Lychee *Litchi chinensis* in soapberry (Sapindaceae) family. Adults seen June–Sep, especially July.

◾ LYCAENIDAE ◾

Fluffy Tit ◾ *Zeltus amasa* 珍灰蝶 WS 30mm

DESCRIPTION Small hairstreak with very long, distinctive wing-tails. Male black above with light blue wing-base; female dark grey with marginal eye-spot. Orangish-brown and white below with two eye-spots and two wing-tails. **DISTRIBUTION** Recent arrival in HK since around 2021, now widely established and uncommon. Not seen in HKI; uncommon in NT and Lantau. Otherwise found from India to southern China, through mainland SE Asia, to Borneo and the Philippines. **HABITAT AND HABITS** Occurs in wooded areas and edges. Active by day. Flight fairly strong at mid-levels. Adults feed on nectar and hold wings closed at rest, except when basking. Caterpillar food plants in HK not well understood, but elsewhere reported on glorybower *Clerodendrum* plants in mint (Lamiaceae) family and *Ixora* plants in coffee (Rubiaceae) family. Adults seen year round.

Male

Male

Female

■ LYCAENIDAE ■

Peacock Royal ■ *Tajuria cippus* 雙尾灰蝶 WS 35–40mm

DESCRIPTION Small hairstreak with black eyes. Dark blue (male) or light blue (female) above with black wing apex. Male has less black than White Royal (p. 156), and female has black submarginal band, lacking in White. Light grey below with broken black line, two orange-crowned eye-spots and two wing-tails. **DISTRIBUTION** Uncommon in HKI and NT; rare in Lantau. Otherwise found from India to southern China, through mainland SE Asia. **HABITAT AND HABITS** Occurs in wooded areas, especially hilltops. Active by day. Flight fairly strong in canopy. Adults feed on nectar and hold wings closed at rest, except when basking. Caterpillars feed on Cinnamon Mistletoe *Scurrula parasitica* and Common Chinese Mistletoe *Macrosolon cochinchinensis* in showy mistletoe (Loranthaceae) family. Adults seen Mar–Dec.

Female

Male

Male

▪ LYCAENIDAE ▪

White Royal ▪ *Pratapa deva* 珀灰蝶 WS 35–40mm

DESCRIPTION Small hairstreak with grey eyes. Dark blue (male) or light blue (female) above with black wing apex. Male has more black than Peacock Royal (p. 155), and female lacks black submarginal band of Peacock. Light grey below with broken black line, two orange-crowned eye-spots and two wing-tails. **DISTRIBUTION** Uncommon. Rare in HKI and Lantau; uncommon in NT. Otherwise found from India to southern China, through mainland SE Asia. **HABITAT AND HABITS** Occurs in wooded areas. Active by day. Flight fairly strong in canopy, and males hilltop. Adults feed on nectar and hold wings closed at rest, except when basking. Caterpillars feed on Cinnamon Mistletoe *Scurrula parasitica* in showy mistletoe (Loranthaceae) family. Adults seen year round.

Male

Spotted Royal ▪ *Tajuria maculata* 豹斑雙尾灰蝶 WS 35–40mm

DESCRIPTION Relatively small hairstreak. Black above with light blue (male) or white (female) patches. White below, with distinctive black spots. Two wing-tails. **DISTRIBUTION** Uncommon. Rare in HKI Island; uncommon in NT; not seen in Lantau. Otherwise found locally from India to southern China, through mainland SE Asia. **HABITAT AND HABITS** Occurs in wooded areas. Active by day. Flight fairly strong. Adults feed on nectar and hold wings closed at rest, except when basking. Unusual in that many eggs are laid together, not just a single egg as in most butterflies. Caterpillar food plants not well understood in HK, but elsewhere feeds on plants in showy mistletoe (Loranthaceae) family. Adults seen May–Nov.

LYCAENIDAE

Broad-tail Royal ▪ *Creon cleobis* 克灰蝶 WS 30–35mm

DESCRIPTION Small hairstreak with grey eyes. Dark blue (male) or light blue (female) with black wing apex. Browner below than Peacock and White Royals (p. 155 and opposite), and line is browner and not broken into segments. Two orange-crowned eye-spots and two wing-tails. **DISTRIBUTION** Rare. Not seen in HKI and Lantau; rare in NT. Otherwise found from India to southern China, through mainland SE Asia. **HABITAT AND HABITS** Occurs in wooded areas. Active by day. Flight fairly strong in canopy, and males hilltop. Adults feed on nectar and hold wings closed at rest, except when basking. Caterpillars feed on Cinnamon Mistletoe *Scurrula parasitica* and Common Chinese Mistletoe *Macrosolon cochinchinensis* in showy mistletoe (Loranthaceae) family. Adults seen year round.

Banded Royal ▪ *Rachana jalindra* 艾灰蝶 WS 40mm

DESCRIPTION Medium-sized hairstreak. Above dark blue with black margins (male) or dark brown with submarginal light blue (female). Distinctive below – white inner half to wing, dark brown outer half, plus two eye-spots and two wing-tails. **DISTRIBUTION** Rare. Not seen in HKI and Lantau; rare in NT. Otherwise found from India to southern China, through mainland SE Asia and the Philippines. **HABITAT AND HABITS** Occurs in wooded areas. Active by day. Flight strong in canopy and males hilltop. Adults feed on nectar and hold wings closed at rest, except when basking. Caterpillar host plants not well understood in HK, but elsewhere feeds on Common Chinese Mistletoe *Macrosolon cochinchinensis* in showy mistletoe (Loranthaceae) family. Adults seen year round except May, Aug and Oct.

▪ Lycaenidae ▪

Chocolate Royal ▪ *Remelana jangala* 萊灰蝶 WS 35mm

DESCRIPTION Small hairstreak with green eyes. Black above with metallic purple (male) or blue (female) patches. Below dark brown (male) or yellowish-brown (female) with thin dark line, two eye-spots (lacking orange) and two wing-tails. Male has metallic blue markings near eye-spots. **DISTRIBUTION** Uncommon in HKI, NT and Lantau. Otherwise found from India to southern China, through mainland SE Asia, to Borneo and the Philippines. **HABITAT AND HABITS** Occurs in wooded and shrubby areas. Active by day. Flight fairly strong. Adults feed on nectar and hold wings closed at rest, except when basking. Caterpillars attended by Rich Spiny Sugar Ants *Polyrhachis dives* and feed on wide variety of plants, including Twin-hanging Embelia *Embelia laeta* in primrose (Primulaceae) family, Pop-gun Seed *Bridelia tomentosa* in spurge (Euphorbiaceae) family, Yellow Cow Wood *Cratoxylum cochinchinense* in St John's wort (Hypericaceae) family and Lance-leaved Sterculia *Sterculia lanceolata* in mallow (Malvaceae) family. Adults seen year round, especially in autumn.

Female

Male

Male

Caterpillar with Polyrhachis *spiny ants*

◾ LYCAENIDAE ◾

Silver Royal ◾ *Ancema blanka* 白襯安灰蝶 WS 30mm

DESCRIPTION Small hairstreak with green eyes. Black above with metallic dark blue (male) or light blue (female). Grey below with thin dark line, two orange-crowned eye-spots and two wing-tails. **DISTRIBUTION** Recent arrival in HK since about 2021, now widely established and uncommon. Rare in HKI and Lantau; uncommon in NT. Otherwise found from India to southern China, through mainland SE Asia to Borneo. **HABITAT AND HABITS** Occurs in wooded and shrubby areas. Active by day. Flight fast and males hilltop. Adults feed on nectar and hold wings closed at rest, except when basking. Caterpillar host plants not well known in HK, but elsewhere feed on Oval Mistletoe *Viscum ovalifolium* in sandalwood (Santalaceae) family. Adults seen year round.

Male

Male

Bi-spot Royal ◾ *Ancema ctesia* 安灰蝶 WS 30–35mm

DESCRIPTION Small hairstreak with green eyes. Black above with metallic blue patches, more turquoise in male and lighter blue in female. Male also with extra black spot in forewing-centre. Grey below with arc of dark dashes (not as linear as in some related species), forewing cell-end bar, two orange-crowned eye-spots and two wing-tails. **DISTRIBUTION** Rare. Not seen in HKI and Lantau; rare in NT. Otherwise found from India to southern China, through mainland SE Asia. **HABITAT AND HABITS** Occurs in wooded and shrubby areas. Active by day and flight fast. Males hilltop and mudpuddle. Adults feed on nectar and hold wings closed at rest, except when basking. Caterpillar host plants not well known in HK, but elsewhere feeds on Jointed Mistletoe *Viscum articulatum* in sandalwood (Santalaceae) family. Adults seen year round.

Male

Male

◾ LYCAENIDAE ◾

Slate Flash ◾ *Rapala manea* 麻燕灰蝶 WS 35mm

Male

DESCRIPTION Small hairstreak with black eyes. Dark metallic purple above (male) or dull purple (female). Brown below with pale arc of darker markings, two eye-spots and one wing-tail. Similar to Cornelian (opposite), but has narrow forewing cell-end bar with only one white border. **DISTRIBUTION** Fairly common in HK Island and NT; uncommon in Lantau. Otherwise found from India to southern China, through mainland SE Asia, to Borneo and the Philippines. **HABITAT AND HABITS** Occurs in wooded areas and gardens. Active by day, and males hilltop. Flight swift. Adults feed on nectar and hold wings closed at rest, except when basking. Caterpillars mainly feed on young leaves and flowers of Glittering-leaved Callerya *Callerya* (*Millettia*) *nitida* in legume (Fabaceae) family. Also reported to feed on wide variety of flowers, including Montane Kudzu *Pueraria montana* (*lobata*), Bentham's Photinia *Photinia benthamiana*, Sweet Viburnum *Viburnum odoratissimum*, Hong Kong Gordonia *Polyspora* (*Gordonia*) *axillaris*, stone oak *Lithocarpus* plants and Hong Kong Orchid Tree *Bauhinia* x *blakeana*. Adults seen year round.

Male

Female

LYCAENIDAE

Cornelian ▪ *Deudorix epijarbas* 玳灰蝶 WS 40mm

DESCRIPTION Medium-sized hairstreak with black eyes. Dark brown above. Male has bright orange patches. Brown below with pale arc of darker markings, two eye-spots and one wing-tail. Similar to Slate Flash (opposite), but has wide forewing cell-end bar with two white borders. **DISTRIBUTION** Uncommon in HKI, NT and Lantau. Otherwise found from India to southern China, through mainland SE Asia, to Borneo and the Philippines. **HABITAT AND HABITS** Occurs in wooded areas and orchards. Active by day. Flight swift. Adults feed on nectar and hold wings closed at rest, except when basking. Unusually, caterpillars mainly feed on fruits, typically young Longan *Dimocarpus longan* and Lychee *Litchi chinensis* in soapberry (Sapindaceae) family. Adults seen Apr–Nov.

Male

Male

Princess Flash ▪ *Deudorix smilis* 斯米玳灰蝶 WS 30–35mm

DESCRIPTION Small hairstreak. Bright blue above with black wing-margins. Brown below with series of darker spots, two eye-spots and one wing-tail. Sexes similar. **DISTRIBUTION** Not previously known in HK, but uncommon since 2019. Not seen in HKI; uncommon in NT; rare in Lantau. Otherwise found locally from southern China, through mainland SE Asia, to Indonesia and northern Australia. **HABITAT AND HABITS** Occurs in wooded areas. Active by day. Flight swift and males hilltop. Adults feed on nectar and hold wings closed at rest, except when basking. Unusually, caterpillars mainly feed on fruits. This is not well understood in HK, but elsewhere known to feed on poison-nut (monkey-orange) *Strychnos* plants in logania (Loganiaceae) family. Adults seen Apr–Dec.

Male

Male

◼ LYCAENIDAE ◼

Green Flash ◼ *Artipe eryx* 綠灰蝶 WS 35–45mm

DESCRIPTION Small to medium hairstreak. Above, black with bright blue patches near base (male) or dark grey with hindwing eye-spots (female). Bright green below, with faint white arc, large black eye-spot and one tail (thin and black in male, large and white in female). **DISTRIBUTION** Uncommon in HKI, NT and Lantau. Otherwise found from central and southern China, through mainland SE Asia. **HABITAT AND HABITS** Occurs in wooded and shrubby areas. Active by day. Flight swift. Adults feed on nectar and hold wings closed at rest, except when basking. Unusually, caterpillars feed on fruits and flowers, typically Common Gardenia *Gardenia jasminoides* and Mountain Pomegranate *Catunarega* (*Randia*) *spinosa* in coffee (Rubiaceae) family. Adults seen Mar–Nov.

Male

Male

Female

Female

■ LYCAENIDAE ■

Broad Spark ■ *Sinthusa chandrana* 生灰蝶 WS 25–30mm

DESCRIPTION Small hairstreak. Above black with metallic blue (male) or dark grey (female). Grey below, with broad, broken arc, two eye-spots and one wing-tail. Male has 2–3 dark basal spots, female one.

Male

Male

DISTRIBUTION Uncommon. Not seen in HKI and Lantau; fairly common in NT. Otherwise found from India to southern China, though mainland SE Asia. **HABITAT AND HABITS** Occurs in wooded and shrubby areas. Active by day. Flight swift and male territorial. Adults feed on nectar and hold wings closed at rest, except when basking. Caterpillars feed on Rusty-haired Raspberry *Rubus reflexus* in rose (Rosaceae) family. Adults seen Feb–Nov.

Narrow Spark ■ *Sinthusa nasaka* 娜生灰蝶 WS 25mm

DESCRIPTION Small hairstreak. Above black with metallic purplish-blue (male) or dark brown (female). Grey below with narrow, unbroken orange arc, two eye-spots and one wing-tail. No basal dark spots, unlike in Broad Spark (above). **DISTRIBUTION** Rare in Hong Kong, especially male. Not seen in HKI and Lantau; rare in NT. Otherwise found from India to southern China, through mainland SE Asia. **HABITAT AND HABITS** Occurs in wooded and shrubby areas. Active by day. Flight swift. Adults feed on nectar and hold wings closed at rest, except when basking. Caterpillar food plants not well understood in HK, but elsewhere known to feed on *Eurya acuminata* in Pentaphylaceae family. Adults seen Mar–May.

Male

Female

Checklist of the Butterflies of Hong Kong

Abbreviations: Hong Kong Status

C	Common	U	Uncommon
FC	Fairly Common	R	Rare

COMMON NAME	SCIENTIFIC NAME	CHINESE NAME	HK STATUS
SWALLOWTAILS (PAPILIONINAE) – 21 HK SPECIES			
SWALLOWTAILS (PAPILIONINAE) – 21 HK SPECIES			
Jays, Swordtails, Bluebottles & Dragontails (Leptocircini) – 6 HK species			
Tailed Jay	*Graphium agamemnon*	統帥青鳳蝶	C
Common Jay	*Graphium doson*	木蘭青鳳蝶	FC
Five-bar Swordtail	*Graphium (Pathysa) antiphates*	綠鳳蝶	U
Common Bluebottle	*Graphium sarpedon*	青鳳蝶	C
Glassy Bluebottle	*Graphium cloanthus*	寬帶青鳳蝶	U
White Dragontail Butterfly	*Lamproptera curius*	燕鳳蝶	U
Birdwings & Pink-bodied Swallowtails (Troidini) – 4 HK species			
Common Rose Swallowtail	*Pachliopta aristolochiae*	紅珠鳳蝶	FC
Chinese Windmill	*Byasa confusa*	中華麝鳳蝶	R
Golden Birdwing	*Troides aeacus*	金裳鳳蝶	U
Common Birdwing	*Troides helena*	裳鳳蝶	U
Typical Swallowtails (Papilionini) – 11 HK species			
Common Mime Swallowtail	*Papilio clytia*	斑鳳蝶	FC
Tawny Mime Swallowtail	*Papilio agestor*	褐斑鳳蝶	U
Common Mormon Swallowtail	*Papilio polytes*	玉帶鳳蝶	C
Great Mormon Swallowtail	*Papilio memnon*	美鳳蝶	C
Spangle Swallowtail	*Papilio protenor*	藍鳳蝶	C
Chinese Peacock Swallowtail	*Papilio bianor*	碧鳳蝶	U
Southern Chinese Peacock Swallowtail	*Papilio dialis*	穹翠鳳蝶	U
Paris Peacock Swallowtail	*Papilio paris*	巴黎翠鳳蝶	C
Red Helen Swallowtail	*Papilio helenus*	玉斑鳳蝶	C
Lime Swallowtail	*Papilio demoleus*	達摩鳳蝶	FC
Chinese Yellow Swallowtail	*Papilio xuthus*	柑橘鳳蝶	FC
SKIPPERS (HESPERIIDAE)			
BASAL SKIPPERS (COELIADINAE) – 10 HK SPECIES			
Indian Awlking	*Choaspes benjaminii*	綠弄蝶	R
Orange Red Skirt	*Choaspes hemixanthus*	半黃綠弄蝶	R
Pale Green Awlet	*Bibasis (Burara) gomata*	白傘弄蝶	U
Branded Orange Awlet	*Bibasis (Burara) oedipodea*	黑斑傘弄蝶	U
Brown Awl	*Badamia exclamationis*	尖翅弄蝶	R
Common Awl	*Hasora badra*	三斑趾弄蝶	U
Slate Awl	*Hasora anura*	無趾弄蝶	R
Common Banded Awl	*Hasora chromus*	雙斑趾弄蝶	U
Plain Banded Awl	*Hasora vitta*	緯帶趾弄蝶	R
White Banded Awl	*Hasora taminatus*	銀針趾弄蝶	R
SPREAD-WING SKIPPERS (PYRGINAE) – 7 HK SPECIES			
Tagiadini – 6 HK species			
Water Snow Flat	*Tagiades litigiosa*	沾邊裙弄蝶	FC
Dark-edged Snow Flat	*Tagiades menaka*	黑邊裙弄蝶	U
White-banded Flat	*Gerosis phisara*	匪夷捷弄蝶	U
Magpie Flat	*Abraximorpha davidii*	白弄蝶	U
Chestnut Banded Angle	*Odontoptilum angulata*	角翅弄蝶	U

◾ Checklist ◾

COMMON NAME	SCIENTIFIC NAME	CHINESE NAME	HK STATUS
Yellow-spotted Angle	*Caprona alida*	白彩弄蝶	U
Celaenorrhinini – 1 HK species			
Common Spotted Flat	*Celaenorrhinus leucocera*	白角星弄蝶	R
GRASS SKIPPERS (HESPERIINAE) – 42 HK SPECIES			
Aeromachini – 7 HK species			
Common Bush Hopper	*Ampittia dioscorides*	黃斑弄蝶	U
Striped Bush Hopper	*Ampittia virgata*	鈎形黃斑弄蝶	U
Grey Scrub Hopper	*Aeromachus jhora*	寬鍔弄蝶	U
Pygmy Scrub Hopper	*Aeromachus pygmaeus*	侏儒鍔弄蝶	R
Moore's Ace	*Halpe porus*	雙子酣弄蝶	R
Monastyrskyi's Ace	*Thoressa monastyrskyi*	黑斑陀弄蝶	R
Tree Flitter	*Hyarotis adrastus*	希弄蝶	U
Erionotini – 5 HK species			
Indian Palm Bob	*Suastus gremius*	素弄蝶	FC
Purple and Gold Flitter	*Zographetus satwa*	黃裳腫脈弄蝶	U
Shiny-spotted Bob	*Isoteinon lamprospilus*	旖弄蝶	R
Common Redeye	*Matapa aria*	瑪弄蝶	U
Rounded Palm-Redeye	*Erionota torus*	黃斑蕉弄蝶	U
Ancistroidini – 4 HK species			
Restricted Demon	*Notocrypta curvifascia*	曲紋袖弄蝶	U
Common Banded Demon	*Notocrypta paralysos*	窄紋袖弄蝶	U
Grass Demon	*Udaspes folus*	薑弄蝶	U
Chestnut Bob	*Iambrix salsala*	雅弄蝶	U
Astictopterini – 1 HK species			
Forest Hopper	*Astictopterus jama*	腌翅弄蝶	FC
Grass Darts & Darters (Taractrocerini) – 11 HK species			
Plain Palm Dart	*Cephrenes acalle*	金斑弄蝶	U
Dark Palm Dart	*Telicota ohara*	黃紋長標弄蝶	R
Hainan Palm Dart	*Telicota besta*	黑脈長標弄蝶	R
Greenish Palm Dart	*Telicota bambusae*	竹长标弄蝶	U
Pale Palm Dart	*Telicota colon*	長標弄蝶	U
Tamil Grass Dart	*Taractrocera ceramas*	草黃弄蝶	R
Common Grass Dart	*Taractrocera maevius*	薇黃弄蝶	R
Lesser Band Dart	*Potanthus trachala*	斷紋黃室弄蝶	U
Indian Band Dart	*Potanthus pseudomaesa*	擬黃室弄蝶	R
Chinese Band Dart	*Potanthus confucius*	孔子黃室弄蝶	U
Yellow Band Dart	*Potanthus pava*	寬紋黃室弄蝶	U
Swifts & Allies (Baorini) – 14 HK species			
Common Straight Swift	*Parnara guttata*	直紋稻弄蝶	U
Continental Swift	*Parnara ganga*	曲紋稻弄蝶	U
Oriental Straight Swift	*Parnara bada*	么紋稻弄蝶	R
Formosan Swift	*Borbo cinnara*	稠弄蝶	C
Bevan's Swift	*Pseudoborbo bevani*	擬稠弄蝶	R
Little Branded Swift	*Pelopidas agna*	南亞穀弄蝶	R
Small Branded Swift	*Pelopidas mathias*	隱紋穀弄蝶	R
Large Branded Swift	*Pelopidas subochracea*	近赭穀弄蝶	R
Great Swift	*Pelopidas assamensis*	印度穀弄蝶	U
Conjoined Swift	*Pelopidas conjuncta*	古銅穀弄蝶	U
Contiguous Swift	*Polytremis lubricans*	黃紋孔弄蝶	U

Checklist

COMMON NAME	SCIENTIFIC NAME	CHINESE NAME	HK STATUS
Paintbrush Swift	*Baoris farri*	刺脛弄蝶	R
Colon Swift	*Caltoris bromus*	斑珂弄蝶	U
Dark Swift	*Caltoris cahira*	珂弄蝶	U
YELLOWS & WHITES (PIERIDAE) – 17 HK SPECIES			
YELLOWS (COLIADINAE) – 6 HK SPECIES			
Euremini – 3 HK species			
Three-spotted Grass Yellow	*Eurema blanda*	檗黃粉蝶	C
Common Grass Yellow	*Eurema hecabe*	寬邊黃粉蝶	C
Broad-bordered Grass Yellow	*Eurema brigitta*	無標黃粉蝶	R
Goniopterygini – 1 HK species			
Tailed Sulphur	*Dercas verhuelli*	檀方粉蝶	U
Coliadini – 2 HK species			
Lemon Emigrant	*Catopsilia pomona*	遷粉蝶	C
Mottled Emigrant	*Catopsilia pyranthe*	梨花遷粉蝶	C
WHITES (PIERINAE) – 11 HK SPECIES			
Colotini – 1 HK species			
Great Orange Tip	*Hebomoia glaucippe*	鶴頂粉蝶	U
Pierini – 10 HK species			
Yellow Orange Tip	*Ixias pyrene*	橙粉蝶	U
Indian Cabbage White	*Pieris canidia*	東方菜粉蝶	C
Small Cabbage White	*Pieris rapae*	菜粉蝶	FC
Common Albatross	*Appias albina*	白翅尖粉蝶	R
Common Gull	*Cepora nerissa*	黑脈園粉蝶	FC
Lesser Gull	*Cepora nadina*	青園粉蝶	U
Spotted Sawtooth	*Prioneris thestylis*	鋸粉蝶	U
Red-based Jezebel	*Delias pasithoe*	報喜斑粉蝶	C
Red-breast Jezebel	*Delias acalis*	紅腋斑粉蝶	R
Painted Jezebel	*Delias hyparete*	優越斑粉蝶	U
BRUSH–FOOTED BUTTERFLIES (NYMPHALIDAE) – 78 HK SPECIES			
MILKWEED BUTTERFLIES (DANAINAE) – 11 HK SPECIES			
Danaini – 11 HK species			
Tiger Butterflies (Danaina) – 8 HK species			
Common Tiger Butterfly	*Danaus genutia*	虎斑蝶	C
Plain Tiger Butterfly	*Danaus chrysippus*	金斑蝶	C
Ceylon Blue Glassy Tiger Butterfly	*Ideopsis similis*	擬旖斑蝶	C
Blue Tiger Butterfly	*Tirumala limniace*	青斑蝶	C
Dark Blue Tiger Butterfly	*Tirumala septentrionis*	嗇青斑蝶	R
Glassy Tiger Butterfly	*Parantica aglea*	絹斑蝶	C
Chestnut Tiger Butterfly	*Parantica sita*	大絹斑蝶	R
Chocolate Tiger Butterfly	*Parantica melaneus*	黑絹斑蝶	R
Euploeina – 3 HK species			
Common Crow Butterfly	*Euploea core*	幻紫斑蝶	FC
Blue-spotted Crow Butterfly	*Euploea midamus*	藍點紫斑蝶	C
Striped Blue Crow Butterfly	*Euploea mulciber*	異型紫斑蝶	U
LEAFWING BUTTERFLIES (CHARAXINAE) – 5 HK SPECIES			
Tawny Rajah	*Charaxes bernardus*	白帶螯蛺蝶	FC
Yellow Rajah	*Charaxes marmax*	螯蛺蝶	R
Common Nawab	*Polyura athamas*	窄斑鳳尾蛺蝶	U
Shan Nawab	*Polyura nepenthes*	忘憂尾蛺蝶	U

Checklist

COMMON NAME	SCIENTIFIC NAME	CHINESE NAME	HK STATUS
Great Nawab	*Polyura eudamippus*	大二尾蛺蝶	R
BROWNS (SATYRINAE) – 17 HK SPECIES			
Elymniini – 1 HK species			
Common Palmfly	*Elymnias hypermnestra*	翠袖鋸眼蝶	C
Amathusiini – 2 HK species			
Large Faun	*Faunis eumeus*	串珠環蝶	C
Common Duffer	*Discophora sondaica*	鳳眼方環蝶	U
Melanitini – 2 HK species			
Common Evening Brown	*Melanitis leda*	暮眼蝶	U
Dark Evening Brown	*Melanitis phedima*	睇暮眼蝶	FC
Satyrs (Satyrini) – 12 HK species			
Dark-branded Bushbrown	*Mycalesis mineus*	小眉眼蝶	C
South China Bushbrown	*Mycalesis mucianus*	平頂眉眼蝶	C
Common Five-Ring	*Ypthima baldus*	矍眼蝶	C
Straight Five-Ring	*Ypthima lisandra*	黎桑矍眼蝶	U
Common Four-Ring	*Ypthima praenubila*	前霧矍眼蝶	U
False Four-Ring	*Ypthima imitans*	擬四眼矍眼蝶	R
Small Three-Ring	*Ypthima norma*	罕矍眼蝶	U
Banded Treebrown	*Lethe confusa*	白帶黛眼蝶	C
Bamboo Treebrown	*Lethe europa*	長紋黛眼蝶	U
Common Treebrown	*Lethe rohria*	波紋黛眼蝶	R
Angled Red Forester	*Lethe chandica*	曲紋黛眼蝶	U
Black-spotted Labyrinth	*Neope muirheadii*	蒙鏈蔭眼蝶	U
FRITILLARIES & ALLIES (HELICONIINAE) – 5 HK SPECIES			
Acraeas (Acraeini) – 1 HK species			
Yellow Coster	*Telchinia (Acraea) issoria*	苧麻珍蝶	U
Longwings (Heliconiini) – 1 HK species			
Red Lacewing Butterfly	*Cethosia biblis*	紅鋸蛺蝶	U
Fritillaries (Argynnini) – 1 HK species			
Tropical Fritillary	*Argynnis (Argyreus) hyperbius*	斐豹蛺蝶	FC
Vagrantini – 2 HK species			
Common Leopard	*Phalanta phalantha*	珐蛺蝶	R
Rustic	*Cupha erymanthis*	黃襟蛺蝶	C
ADMIRALS (LIMENITIDINAE) – 21 HK SPECIES			
Sailers (Neptini) – 8 HK species			
Short Banded Sailer	*Phaedyma columella*	柱菲蛺蝶	FC
Common Sailer	*Neptis hylas*	中環蛺蝶	C
Southern Sullied Sailer	*Neptis clinia*	珂環蛺蝶	FC
Sullied Brown Sailer	*Neptis nata*	娜環蛺蝶	U
Cream-spotted Sailer	*Neptis soma*	娑環蛺蝶	R
Plain Sailer	*Neptis cartica*	卡環蛺蝶	R
Small Yellow Sailer	*Neptis miah*	彌環蛺蝶	U
Common Lascar	*Pantoporia hordonia*	金蟠蛺蝶	U
Sergeants (Limenitidini) – 8 HK species			
Colour Sergeant	*Athyma nefte*	相思帶蛺蝶	C
Orange Staff Sergeant	*Athyma cama*	雙色帶蛺蝶	R
Common Sergeant	*Athyma perius*	玄珠帶蛺蝶	U
Blackvein Sergeant	*Athyma ranga*	離斑帶蛺蝶	U
Staff Sergeant	*Athyma selenophora*	新月帶蛺蝶	FC

Checklist

COMMON NAME	SCIENTIFIC NAME	CHINESE NAME	HK STATUS
Five-dot Sergeant	Limenitis (Parathyma) sulpitia	殘鍔線蛺蝶	FC
White Commodore	Parasarpa dudu	丫紋俳蛺蝶	U
Commander	Moduza procris	穆蛺蝶	U
Barons (Adoliadini) – 5 HK species			
Gaudy Baron	Euthalia lubentina	紅斑翠蛺蝶	U
Common Baron	Euthalia aconthea	矛翠蛺蝶	U
White-edged Blue Baron	Euthalia phemius	尖翅翠蛺蝶	FC
Green Skirt Baron	Tanaecia (Cynitia) whiteheadi	綠裙蛺蝶	U
Common Archduke	Lexias pardalis	小豹律蛺蝶	C
Castors (Biblidinae) – 1 HK species			
Angled Castor	Ariadne ariadne	波蛺蝶	U
EMPERORS (APATURINAE) – 4 HK SPECIES			
Red Ring Skirt	Hestina assimilis	黑脈蛺蝶	FC
Black Prince	Rohana parisatis	羅蛺蝶	U
Courtesan	Euripus nyctelius	芒蛺蝶	U
Eastern Courtier	Sephisa chandra	帥蛺蝶	R
MAP BUTTERFLIES (CYRESTINAE) – 2 HK SPECIES			
Constable	Dichorragia nesimachus	電蛺蝶	U
Common Mapwing	Cyrestis thyodamas	網絲蛺蝶	C
ANGLEWINGS, EGGFLIES & PANSIES (NYMPHALINAE) – 12 HK SPECIES			
Anglewings (Nymphalini) – 5 HK species			
Blue Admiral	Kaniska canace	琉璃蛺蝶	U
Asian Comma	Polygonia c-aureum	黃鉤蛺蝶	R
Painted Lady	Vanessa cardui	小紅蛺蝶	U
Indian Red Admiral	Vanessa indica	大紅蛺蝶	U
Common Jester	Symbrenthia lilaea	散紋盛蛺蝶	C
Eggflies & Pansies (Junoniini) – 7 HK species			
Danaid Eggfly	Hypolimnas misippus	金斑蛺蝶	U
Great Eggfly	Hypolimnas bolina	幻紫斑蛺蝶	C
Blue Pansy	Junonia orithya	翠藍眼蛺蝶	U
Lemon Pansy	Junonia lemonias	蛇眼蛺蝶	C
Grey Pansy	Junonia atlites	波紋眼蛺蝶	U
Peacock Pansy	Junonia almana	美眼蛺蝶	U
Chocolate Pansy	Junonia iphita	鉤翅眼蛺蝶	C
METALMARKS (RIODINIDAE) – 3 HK SPECIES			
Punchinello	Zemeros flegyas	波蜆蝶	C
Plum Judy	Abisara echerius	蛇目褐蜆蝶	C
Orange Punch	Dodona egeon	大斑尾蜆蝶	U
LYCAENIDAE (GOSSAMER-WINGED BUTTERFLIES) – 57 HK SPECIES			
SUNBEAMS (CURETINAE) – 1 HK SPECIES			
Angled Sunbeam	Curetis acuta (dentata)	尖翅銀灰蝶	U
HARVESTERS (MILETINAE) – 2 HK SPECIES			
Forest Pierrot	Taraka hamada	蚜灰蝶	U
Common Brownie	Miletus chinensis	中華雲灰蝶	R
SILVERLINES (APHNAEINAE) – 2 HK SPECIES			
Long-banded Silverline	Cigaritis (Spindasis) lohita	銀線灰蝶	U
Club Silverline	Cigaritis (Spindasis) syama	豆粒銀線灰蝶	U
COPPERS (LYCAENINAE) – 1 HK SPECIES			
Purple Sapphire	Heliophorus epicles	彩灰蝶	C

■ Checklist ■

COMMON NAME	SCIENTIFIC NAME	CHINESE NAME	HK STATUS
BLUES (POLYOMMATINAE) – 28 HK SPECIES			
Typical Blues (Polyommatini) – 28 HK species			
Danina – 4 HK species			
Tailless Line Blue	*Prosotas dubiosa*	疑波灰蝶	FC
Common Line Blue	*Prosotas nora*	娜拉波灰蝶	U
Transparent Six-line Blue	*Nacaduba kurava*	古樓娜灰蝶	FC
Rounded Six-line Blue	*Nacaduba berenice*	百娜灰蝶	U
Jamidina – 3 HK species			
Common Cerulean	*Jamides celeno*	錫冷雅灰蝶	U
Dark Cerulean	*Jamides bochus*	雅灰蝶	FC
Metallic Cerulean	*Jamides alecto*	素雅灰蝶	FC
Lampidina – 1 HK species			
Pea Blue	*Lampides boeticus*	亮灰蝶	C
Catochrysopsina – 2 HK species			
Forget-Me-Not	*Catochrysops strabo*	咖灰蝶	FC
Silver Forget-Me-Not	*Catochrysops panormus*	藍咖灰蝶	R
Oboroniina – 1 HK species			
Gram Blue	*Euchrysops cnejus*	棕灰蝶	U
Everina – 1 HK species			
Orange-tipped Pea-Blue	*Everes lacturnus*	長尾藍灰蝶	U
Polyommatina – 3 HK species			
Plains Cupid	*Luthrodes (Chilades) pandava*	曲紋紫灰蝶	C
Jewelled Grass-Blue	*Freyeria (Chilades) putli*	普紫灰蝶	U
Lime Blue	*Chilades lajus*	紫灰蝶	FC
Leptotina – 1 HK species			
Zebra Blue	*Leptotes (Syntarucus) plinius*	細灰蝶	R
Lycaenopsina – 6 HK species			
Common Hedge Blue	*Acytolepis puspa*	鈕灰蝶	C
Plain Hedge Blue	*Celastrina lavendularis*	薰衣琉璃灰蝶	U
Pale Hedge Blue	*Udara dilecta*	嫵灰蝶	R
Albocerulean	*Udara albocaerulea*	白斑嫵灰蝶	R
Malayan	*Megisba malaya*	美姬灰蝶	U
Quaker	*Neopithecops zalmora*	一點灰蝶	U
Pithecopina – 1 HK species			
Forest Quaker	*Pithecops corvus*	黑丸灰蝶	U
Fameganina – 1 HK species			
Black-spotted Grass Blue	*Famegana nisa (alsulus)*	珐灰蝶	U
Zizeeriina – 3 HK species			
Pale Grass Blue	*Pseudozizeeria (Zizeeria) maha*	酢漿灰蝶	C
Dark Grass Blue	*Zizeeria karsandra*	吉灰蝶	R
Lesser Grass Blue	*Zizina otis*	毛眼灰蝶	FC
Brephidiina – 1 HK species			
Tiny Grass Blue	*Zizula hylax*	長腹灰蝶	U
HAIRSTREAKS (THECLINAE) – 23 HK SPECIES			
Amblypodiini – 1 HK species			
Silverstreak Blue	*Iraota timoleon*	鐵木萊異灰蝶	FC
Arhopalini – 5 HK species			
Falcate Oakblue	*Mahathala ameria*	瑪灰蝶	U
Powdered Oakblue	*Arhopala bazalus*	百嬈灰蝶	U

169

Checklist

COMMON NAME	SCIENTIFIC NAME	CHINESE NAME	HK STATUS
Dull Oakblue	Arhopala centaurus	銀鏈嬈灰蝶	R
Hooked Oakblue	Arhopala paramuta	小嬈灰蝶	R
Burmese Bushblue	Arhopala birmana	緬甸嬈灰蝶	U
Horagini – 2 HK species			
Common Onyx	Horaga onyx	斑灰蝶	U
Violet Onyx	Horaga albimacula	白斑灰蝶	R
Hypolycaenini – 1 HK species			
Fluffy Tit	Zeltus amasa	珍灰蝶	U
Iolaini – 5 HK species			
Spotted Royal	Tajuria maculata	豹斑雙尾灰蝶	U
Peacock Royal	Tajuria cippus	雙尾灰蝶	U
White Royal	Pratapa deva	珀灰蝶	U
Broad-tail Royal	Creon cleobis	克灰蝶	R
Banded Royal	Rachana jalindra	艾灰蝶	R
Remelanini – 3 HK species			
Chocolate Royal	Remelana jangala	萊灰蝶	U
Silver Royal	Ancema blanka	"白襯安灰蝶"	U
Bi-spot Royal	Ancema ctesia	安灰蝶	R
Deudorigini – 6 HK species			
Slate Flash	Rapala manea	麻燕灰蝶	FC
Cornelian	Deudorix epijarbas	玳灰蝶	U
Princess Flash	Deudorix smilis	斯米玳灰蝶	U
Green Flash	Artipe eryx	綠灰蝶	U
Broad Spark	Sinthusa chandrana	生灰蝶	U
Narrow Spark	Sinthusa nasaka	娜生灰蝶	R

VAGRANTS & OTHER RARE SPECIES			OBSERVATIONS
SWALLOWTAILS (PAPILIONIDAE)			
Four-bar Swordtail	Graphium agetes	斜紋綠鳳蝶	1
Six-bar Swordtail	Graphium eurous	升天鳳蝶	1
Veined Jay	Graphium chironides	碎斑青鳳蝶	1
Old World Swallowtail	Papilio machaon	金鳳蝶	0
SKIPPERS (HESPERIIDAE)			
Beggar's Ace	Halpe paupera	珀酣弄蝶	1
Common Orange Awlet	Bibasis (Burara) jaina	橙翅傘弄蝶	0
WHITES AND YELLOWS (PIERIDAE)			
Redspot Sawtooth	Prioneris philonome	紅肩鋸粉蝶	6
Chocolate Albatross	Appias lyncida	紅肩鋸粉蝶	4
Colias poliographus	Colias poliographus	東亞豆粉蝶	2
Psyche	Leptosia nina	纖粉蝶	1
Spotless Grass Yellow	Eurema laeta	尖角黃粉蝶	0
Hill Jezebel	Delias belladonna	艷婦斑粉蝶	0
BRUSH-FOOTED BUTTERFLIES (NYMPHALIDAE)			
Yellow Pansy	Junonia hierta	黃裳眼蛺蝶	5
Orange Oakleaf	Kallima inachus	枯葉蛺蝶	4
Tailed Rustic	Vagrans egista	彩蛺蝶	4
Straight-banded Treebrown	Lethe verma	玉帶黛眼蝶	3
European Peacock Butterfly	Aglais io	孔雀蛺蝶	3

VAGRANTS & OTHER RARE SPECIES

VAGRANTS & OTHER RARE SPECIES			OBSERVATIONS
Swinhoe's Chocolate Tiger	*Parantica swinhoei*	史氏絹斑蝶	3
Common Yeoman	*Cirrochroa tyche*	幸運輯蛺蝶	2
China Nawab	*Polyura narcaea*	二尾蛺蝶	2
Club Beak	*Libythea myrrha*	棒紋喙蝶	1
Malayan Eggfly	*Hypolimnas anomala*	八重山紫蛺蝶	1
Double-branded Crow	*Euploea sylvester*	雙標紫斑蝶	0
Australian Lurcher	*Yoma sabina*	瑤蛺蝶	0
GOSSAMER-WINGED BUTTERFLIES (LYCAENIDAE)			
Tongeia filicaudis	*Tongeia filicaudis*	點玄灰蝶	5
Small Copper	*Lycaena phlaeas*	紅灰蝶	3
Short-tailed Blue	*Cupido argiades*	霧社燕小灰蝶	2
Dark Himalayan Oak Blue	*Arhopala rama*	齒翅嬈灰蝶	0

Data from iNaturalist: research-grade observations as of October 2023.

PHOTO CREDITS

Main descriptions: photos are denoted by a page number followed by t (top), m (middle), b (bottom), l (left) or r (right).

John Allcock 90bl, 163br. **Keith Chan** 46b, 163tl. **To Chan** 104t, 104bl. **Lam Lai Cheng** 24t, 162bl. **W. K. Cheng** 9bl, 9br, 10m, 15tr, 15bl, 16b, 17tl, 17tr, 17ml, 17bl, 18ml, 19tr, 19br, 20mr, 20b, 21bl, 21br, 22tl, 22tr, 22bl, 22br, 23t, 23m, 23b, 24bm, 25bl, 26tl, 29tl, 29tr, 29b, 30tr, 30ml, 30bl, 31bl, 34br, 35t, 35bl, 35br, 36t, 37t, 37bl, 38t, 38bl, 38br, 39tl, 39tm, 39tr, 39br, 40b, 41t, 41b, 42tl, 48b, 49tl, 49tr, 49b, 50tl, 57bl, 57br, 60tl, 60ml, 60br, 62tl, 62tr, 62b, 65tl, 65tr, 65br, 66tl, 66br, 67tr, 67bl, 67br, 68tr, 70t, 71t, 72m, 72bm, 72b, 74t, 74br, 75bl, 77t, 77bl, 77br, 79t, 79b, 80t, 80bl, 81tr, 81mr, 85t, 85m, 90br, 91t, 91br, 92bl, 93br, 93tr, 94bl, 97t, 97b, 102tl, 102ml, 102bl, 102br, 103tl, 103tr, 103br, 105br, 107mr, 109tl, 110t, 110br, 111tl, 111tm, 111tr, 111bl, 112tl, 112tr, 114bl, 114br, 115bl, 117t, 117br, 118t, 118br, 119tr, 119br, 120tl, 120tr, 121br, 123t, 123bl, 123br, 124br, 125t, 126bl, 126br, 127bl, 128b, 129t, 129b, 130t, 134b, 140b, 141t, 141bl, 143bl, 143br, 144t, 147tl, 147tr, 147bl, 149tl, 151tl, 151b, 152t, 153tl, 153tr, 155bl, 158tl, 158tr, 162bl. **Rance Cheung** 54bl. **Eric Ching** 27b, 90bm, 134tl, 158br, 161tl. **Indiana Cristo** 9tl. **Janchai Delecate** 116t. **Tree Fong** 54t, 132b, 151tr, 155br, 156t, 159bl, 159br. **Andrew Hardacre** 9tr, 16tl, 16tr, 128tr, 150tr, 160t. **Tommy Hui** 163bl. **Alan Kwok and Ada Tai** 4r, 10l, 21t, 23bm, 24bl, 25t, 26tr, 31t, 32tl, 33t, 33b, 34bl, 41b, 44br, 50br, 51t, 66t, 68tl, 68b, 71b, 72t, 73t, 74bl, 75br, 76tl, 76tm, 78t, 78b, 80br, 82b, 83m, 83b, 84b, 85b, 87br, 88bl, 95tr, 95bl, 96br, 98tl, 98tr, 98b, 99t, 99bl, 105tr, 105bm, 106tr, 106bl, 107tr, 107bl, 108tl, 108ml, 108bl, 109bl, 109br, 110bl, 112bl, 113bl, 113br, 114tl, 115tl, 115br, 117bl, 118bl, 121tl, 122tl, 122br, 124tl, 124tm, 124tr, 125br, 126tl, 126ml, 127br, 139t, 142b. **Andrew Lai** 89tl. **Crystal Lam** 10r, 55t, 90tl, 101tr, 131bl, 133t, 138bl, 140tr, 146t, 150tl, 152bl, 154t, 154bl, 159tl, 161br, 162tl. **Alice Lee** 90tr. **Cody Lee** 59bm. **Setsuna Leung** 153br. **Jimmy Li** 163tr. **K. W. Liu** 15tl, 15br, 18t, 19tl, 19bl, 20t, 20ml, 24br, 25br, 26bl, 26br, 30tl, 31br, 34t, 36bl, 36bm, 36br, 39bl, 40tl, 40tm, 40tr, 42tr, 42b, 43tl, 43tr, 44tl, 44tr, 44bl, 45t, 45bl, 45br, 46t, 47t, 47bl, 48t, 48m, 50tr, 50bl, 51m, 51bm, 51b, 52t, 52m, 52bm, 52b, 53mr, 54br, 55bl, 55br, 56t, 56b, 58tl, 58tr, 58bl, 58br, 59tl, 59tr, 59br, 60bl, 61tr, 61br, 61tl, 61bl, 63t, 63bl, 63br, 64tl, 64tr, 64ml, 64bl, 65bl, 67mr, 69m, 69b, 70m, 70b, 81bl, 81br, 82t, 83t, 84t, 86t, 86bl, 86br, 87t, 87bl, 88t, 88br, 89tr, 91bl, 92br, 93br, 94t, 94br, 95tl, 95br, 96ml, 96bl, 97br, 100t, 100b, 101tl, 101bl, 103bl, 105tl, 105bl, 106tl, 106br, 107br, 111br, 113tl, 113tr, 114tr, 120mr, 120br, 121tr, 121bl, 122tr, 122bl, 124bl, 125bl, 127tl, 127tl, 127tr, 128tl, 130b, 131tl, 131br, 132t, 135t, 135b, 136t, 136bl, 136br, 137tl, 137bl, 138tl, 138tr, 138br, 142tl, 142tr, 145tl, 145tm, 145tr, 145b, 147tm, 147br, 148tl, 149b, 154br. **Scott Lo** 160br. **Jason Mann** 4l, 112br. **Bergman Ng** 89bl. **Pasteur Ng** 93tl, 119bl, 144br, 156bl, 156br, 161bl. **Stephen Ng** 18bl, 28t, 28bl, 32tr, 32b, 53tl, 59bl, 69t, 75t, 76bl, 76br, 92tl, 96tl, 101bt, 108tr, 109tr, 115tr, 133b, 134tr, 137tm, 137tr, 137br, 139tl, 140tl, 141br, 143t, 144bl, 146b, 148tr, 148b, 149tr, 150bl, 150br, 152br, 153bl, 157t, 157b, 158bl, 159tr, 160bl. **Poonpoon** 89br. **Tommy Swift** 28br. **Catalina Tong** 162tr. **Tsui Ka Pui** 27r. **Zit Verdin** 155t. **Timmy Wong** 57t. **Charmian Woodhouse** 139br. **Jonathan Yang** 53tr, 92ml, 161tr. **Yu Ching Tam** 119mr. **Ling Yuet Yin** 18br, 116b.

171

■ Acknowledgements ■

Thank you to John Beaufoy and Rosemary Wilkinson for the suggestion to write this book, as well as excellent editorial support. Thank you to the creators, supporters and users of iNaturalist, a powerful tool for identification and connection with other outdoor enthusiasts around the world. I express great appreciation for the photographers who donated their hard-earned images to make this book come alive. Special thanks to W. K. Cheng, K. W. Liu, Alan Kwok and Ada Tai, Stephen Ng, Crystal Lam and others detailed below for outstanding contributions.

Thank you to my parents, who said 'yes' to a nine-year-old boy interested in joining a nature walk at Hong Kong's Mai Po Reserve. Along with learning to love China, they allowed me to spend innumerable hours outdoors, and as a 12 year old I remember leaving well before dawn on a solo visit to Tai Po Kau Nature Reserve, to explore and indulge an apparently boundless curiosity. Thank you to my first science teachers Cheri Mann, Mrs McHenry, Mr Krysl, Mr Ley and Mrs Wilder, for helping me to grow. To Ms Liu (刘老师) in Changchun, to my great uncle John, who sent me books in China and helped support my curiosity. To Larry Parmeter for allowing me to join him on hikes as a young teenager. To actor Hugh O'Brian for encouragement, to US Senator Alan K. Simpson, the Hearst family and philanthropist Walter Annenberg, without whose financial support I could not have attended Harvard College. His handwritten letters were formative for my life. I'm grateful for the chance of meeting Li Ka-shing and Tung Chee-hwa in college, which increased my interest in Hong Kong. To my undergraduate advisor Benjamin L. Ebert, MD, DPhil, Professors Dudley Herschbach and Tu Weiming, thesis advisor and Harvard-Yenching Institute Director Elizabeth J. Perry, blood-disease expert Carlo Brugnara, MD at Boston Children's Hospital, Terence Dermody, MD, and my cancer research PhD advisor and President of the American Association for Cancer Research, Raymond DuBois MD, PhD. To Nigel Redman for introducing John Beaufoy. To Paul Farmer, MD, PhD, the Hong Kong University library, and local lepidoptery expert Roger Kendrick. To my boss's boss Peter Ma Mingzhi, who founded and scaled a business, Ping An Insurance, which has positively impacted hundreds of millions of people. To my friend and supporter, respected mammologist and Research Head at the Australian Museum Dr Kristofer Helgen, who I expect will discover more new mammal species than anyone alive today. Each of you played a key role in my life and in making this book possible. To my siblings and extended family, and hundreds of others who played a part in making this book what it is. Thank you.

Most of all, thank you to my lovely wife Natalie, mariposa. Without your love and encouragement, this book would not exist. And to our children Jason, Abigail Lily, Shiloh and Fern Mann. May you and your generation enjoy and care for butterflies and the interconnected web of life, on which we all depend, even better than we did.

While every effort has been made to ensure the accuracy of the information in this book, the author takes responsibility for any errors. Please send corrections, to be updated in a future edition, to NGButterfliesHK@gmail.com.

Acknowledgements

ONLINE REFERENCES

iNaturalist: Online platform to post photographs and receive help with identification of butterflies and other life forms. Perhaps the most easily accessible and powerful resource listed here. www.inaturalist.org

Hong Kong Lepidopterists' Society: www.hkls.org

Butterfly webpage on HK Special Administrative Region Agriculture, Fisheries and Conservation Department website: www.afcd.gov.hk/english/conservation/hkbiodiversity/speciesgroup/speciesgroup_butterflies.html

Butterflies of Indochina website: https://yutaka.it-n.jp

PUBLICATIONS

Bascombe, Mike, Johnston, Gweneth & Bascombe, Frieda. 1999. *The Butterflies of Hong Kong*. Princeton University Press.

Dudgeon, David & Corlett, Richard. 1994. *Hills and Streams: An Ecology of Hong Kong*. Hong Kong University Press.

Kirton, Laurence. 2021. *A Naturalist's Guide to the Butterflies of Peninsular Malaysia, Singapore & Thailand*. John Beaufoy Publishing.

Lin, Yueh-Hsien & Liao, Yi-Chang & Yang, Chin-Cheng & Billen, Johan & Yang, Man-Miao & Hsu, Yu-Feng. 2019. Vibrational communication between a myrmecophilous butterfly *Spindasis lohita* (Lepidoptera: Lycaenidae) and its host ant *Crematogaster rogenhoferi* (Hymenoptera: Formicidae). *Scientific Reports*. 9. 10.1038/s41598-019-54966-6.

Lo, Philip & Hsu, Yu-Feng & Pun, Sui-Fai. 2020. First verifiable record of *Neptis nata* Moore, 1857 (Lepidoptera, Nymphalidae) in Hong Kong. *Butterflies*. 54–55.

Lo, Y. F. & Hui W. L. 2004. *Hong Kong Butterflies*. Cosmos Books & Friends of the Country Parks, Hong Kong.

Lo, Philip & Hui, Wing-leung. 2006. The second *Nacaduba* Moore, 1881 species found in Hong Kong with notes on its diagnostic features, distribution and host association (Lepidoptera: Lycaenidae). *Entomologische Zeitschrift Stuttgart* 116(2). 66–70.

Pun Sui Fai & Yeung Ying Ho. 2012. *Encyclopedia of Hong Kong Butterflies. Butterfly Identification*. Hong Kong Lepidoptera Society Limited.

Pun Sui Fai. 2015. *Hong Kong Butterfly Watching Manual, Advanced Edition*. Environmental Protection Council Fung Yuen Butterfly Conservation Area.

Smetacek, Peter. 2017. *A Naturalist's Guide to the Butterflies of India*. John Beaufoy Publishing.

Toussaint, Emmanuel & Breinholt, Jesse & Earl, Chandra & Warren, Andrew & Brower, Andrew & Yago, Masaya & Dexter, Kelly & Espeland, Marianne & Pierce, Naomi & Lohman, David & Kawahara, Akito. 2018. Anchored phylogenomics illuminates the skipper butterfly tree of life. *BMC Evolutionary Biology*.

Index

Abisara echerius 127
Abraximorpha davidii 34
  virgata 37
Ace, Monastyrskyi's 38
  Moore's 38
Acytolepis puspa 142
Admiral, Blue 118
  Indian Red 120
Aeromachus jhora 37
  pygmaeus 38
Albatross, Common 67
Albocerulean 144
Ampittia dioscorides 36
Ancema blanka 159
  ctesia 159
Angle, Chestnut
    Banded 35
  Yellow-spotted 35
Appias albina 67
Archduke, Common 112
Arhopala bazalus 151
  birmana 152
  centaurus (pseudocentaurus) 151
  paramuta 152
Ariadne ariadne 111
Argynnis (Argyreus) hyperbius 95
Artipe eryx 162
Astictopterus jama 44
Athyma cama 104
  nefte 103
  perius 105
  ranga 105
  selenophora 106
Awl, Brown 30
  Common 30
  Common Banded 31
  Plain Banded 32
  Slate 31
  White Banded 32
Awkling, Indian 27
Awlet, Banded Orange 29
  Pale Green 29

Badamia exclamationis 30
Band Dart, Chinese 51
  Indian 50
  Lesser 50
  Yellow 50
Baron, Common 108
  Gaudy 109
  Green Skirt 111
  White-edged Blue 110
Bibasis (Burara) gomata 29
  (Burara) oedipodea 29
Birdwing, Common 19
  Golden 19
Black Prince 113
Bluebottle, Common 16
  Glassy 17
Blue, Gram 138
  Lime 141
  Pea 136
  Silverstreak 150
  Zebra 140
Bob, Chestnut 44
  Indian Palm 40
  Shiny-spotted 41
Borbo cinnara 53
Branded Swift,
  Large 57
  Little 55
  Small 56
Brownie, Common 129
Bushblue, Burmese 152
Bushbrown, Dark-branded 86
  South China 87
Bush Hopper,
  Common 36
  Striped 37
Byasa confusa 17

Cabbage White,
  Indian 66
  Small 67
Caltoris bromus 60
  cahira 60

Caprona alida 35
Castor, Angled 111
Catochrysops panormus 137
  strabo 137
Catopsilia pomona 63
  pyranthe 64
Celaenorrhinus leucocera 36
Celastrina lavendularis 143
Cephrenes acalle 45
Cepora nadina 69
  nerissa 68
Cerulean, Common 134
  Dark 135
  Metallic 135
Cethosia biblis 94
Charaxes bernardus 80
  marmax 81
Chilades lajus 141
Choaspes benjaminii 27
  hemixanthus 28
Cigaritis (Spindasis) lohita 130
  syama 131
Comma, Asian 119
Commander, 108
Commodore, White 107
Constable 117
Cornelian 161
Coster, Yellow 93
Courtesan 115
Courtier, Eastern 116
Creon cleobis 157
Crow Butterfly, Blue-spotted 78
  Common 77
  Striped Blue 79
Cupha erymanthis 96
Cupid, Plains 139
Curetis acuta (dentata) 128
Cyrestis thyodamas 117

Danaus chrysippus 72
  genutia 72
Delias acalis 71

  hyparete 71
  pasithoe 70
Demon, Common
    Banded 43
  Grass 43
  Restricted 42
Dercas verhuelli 62
Deudorix epijarbas 161
  smilis 161
Dichorragia nesimachus 117
Discophora sondaica 84
Dodona egeon 127
Dragontail Butterfly,
  White 17
Duffer, Common 84

Eggfly, Danaid 121
  Great 122
Elymnias hypermnestra 83
Emigrant, Lemon 63
  Mottled 64
Erionota torus 42
Euchrysops cnejus 138
Euploea core 77
  midamus 78
  mulciber 79
Eurema blanda 61
  brigitta 62
  hecabe 61
  laeta 62
Euripus nyctelius 115
Euthalia aconthea 108
  lubentina 109
  phemius 110
Evening Brown,
  Common 85
  Dark 85
Everes lacturnus 138

Famegana nisa (alsulus) 146
Faun, Large 83
Faunis eumeus 83
Five-Ring, Common 88
  Straight 89
Flash, Green 162
  Princess 161

Index

Slate 160
Flat, Common Spotted 36
  Magpie 34
  White-banded 34
Flitter, Purple and Gold 40
  Tree 39
Forester, Angled Red 92
Forget-Me-Not 137
  Silver 137
Four-Ring, Common 89
  False 90
Freyeria (*Chilades*) *putli* 140
Fritillary, Tropical 95

Gerosis phisara 34
Graphium agamemnon 14
  (*Pathysa*) *antiphates* 15
  aristolochiae 17
  cloanthus 16
  curius 16
  doson 14
  sarpedon 15
Grass Blue, Black-spotted 146
  Dark 148
  Jewelled 140
  Lesser 149
  Pale 147
  Tiny 149
Grass Dart, Common 49
  Tamil 49
Grass Yellow, Broad-bordered 62
  Common 61
  Spotless 62
  Three-spotted 62
Gull, Common 68
  Lesser 69

Halpe porus 38
Hasora anuraa 31
  badra 30
  chromus 31

  taminatus 32
  vitta 32
Hebomoia glaucippe 64
Hedge Blue, Common 142
  Pale 144
  Plain 143
Heliophorus epicles 131
Hestina assimilis 114
Hopper, Forest 44
Horaga albimacula 153
  onyx 153
Hyarotis adrastus 39
Hypolimnas bolina 122
  misippus 121

Iambrix salsala 44
Ideopsis similis 73
Iraota timoleon 150
Isoteinon lamprospilus 41
Ixias pyrene 65

Jamides alecto 135
  bochus 135
  celeno 134
Jay, Common 15
  Tailed 15
Jester, Common 120
Jezebel, Painted 71
  Red-based 70
  Red-breast 71
Junonia almana 125
  atlites 124
  iphita 126
  lemonias 124
  orithya 123

Kaniska canace 118

Labyrinth, Black-spotted 93
Lacewing Butterfly, Red 94
Lampides boeticus 136
Lascar, Common 102
Leopard, Common 96
Leptotes (*Syntarucus*) *plinius* 140

Lethe chandica 92
  confusa 91
  europa 91
  rohria 92
Lexias pardalis 112
Limenitis (*Parathyma*) *sulpitia* 107
Line Blue, Common 132
  Tailless 132
Luthrodes (*Chilades*) *pandava* 139

Mahathala ameria 150
Malayan 145
Mapwing, Common 117
Matapa aria 41
Megisba malaya 145
Melanitis leda 85
  phedima 85
Miletus chinensis 129
Moduza procris 108
Mycalesis mineus 86
  mucianus (*zonata*) 87

Nacaduba berenice 134
  kurava 133
Nawab, Common 81
  Great 82
  Shan 82
Neope muirheadii 93
Neopithecops zalmora 145
Neptis cartica 101
  clinia 99
  hylas 98
  miah 102
  nata 101
  soma 100
Notocrypta curvifascia 42
  paralysos 43

Oakblue, Dull 151
  Falcate 150
  Hooked 152
  Powdered 151
Odontoptilum angulata 35

Onyx, Common 153
  Violet 153
Orange Tip, Great 64
  Yellow 65

Painted Lady 119
Palm Dart, Dark 46
  Greenish 48
  Hainan 47
  Pale 48
  Plain 45
Palmfly, Common 83
Palm-Redeye, Rounded 42
Panara bada 53
  ganga 52
  guttata 52
Pansy, Blue 123
  Chocolate 126
  Grey 124
  Lemon 124
  Peacock 125
Pantoporia hordonia 202
Papilio agestor 20
  bianor 23
  clytia 18
  demoleus 26
  dialis 28
  helenus 25
  memnon 22
  paris 24
  polytes 21
  protenor 23
  xuthus 26
Parantica aglea 75
  melaneus 76
  sita 76
Parasarpa dudu 107
Pea-Blue, Orange-tipped 138
Pelopidas agna 55
  assamensis 58
  conjuncta 58
  farri 59
  lubricans 59
  mathias 56
  subochracea 57
Phaedyma columella 97
Phalanta phalantha 96

Index

Pieris canidia 66
   rapae 67
Pierrot, Forest 129
Pithecops corvus 146
Plum Judy 127
Polygonia c-aureum 119
Polyura athamas 81
   eudamippus 82
   nepenthes 82
Potanthus confucius 51
   pava 51
   pseudomaesa 50
   trachala 50
Pratapa deva 156
Prioneris thestylis 70
Prosotas dubiosa 132
   nora 132
Pseudoborbo bevani 54
Pseudozizeeria
   (*Zizeeria*) *maha* 147
Punch, Orange 127
Punchinello 126

Quaker 145
   Forest 146

Rachana jalindra 157
Rajah, Tawny 80
   Yellow 81
Rapala manea 160
Redeye, Common 41
Remelana jangala 158
Rohana parisatis 113
Royal, Banded 157
   Bi-spot 159
   Broad-tail 157
   Chocolate 158
   Peacock 155
   Silver 159
   Spotted 156
   White 156
Rustic 96

Sailer, Common 98
   Cream-spotted 100
   Plain 101
   Short Banded 97
   Small Yellow 102
   Southern Sullied 99
   Sullied Brown 101
Sapphire, Purple 131
Sawtooth, Spotted 70
Scrub Hopper, Grey 37
   Pygmy 38
   Striped 37
Sephisa chandra 116
Sergeant, Blackvein 105
   Colour 103
   Common 105
   Five-dot 107
Silverline, Club 131
   Long-banded 130
Sinthusa chandrana 163
   nasaka 163
Six-line Blue, Rounded 134
   Transparent 133
Skirt, Orange Red 114
   Red Ring 28
Snow Flat, Dark-edged 33
   Water 33
Spark, Broad 163
   Narrow 163
Staff Sergeant 106
   Orange 104
Straight Swift,
   Common 52
   Oriental 53
Suastus gremius 40
Sulphur, Tailed 62
Sunbeam, Angled 128
Swallowtail, Chinese
   Peacock 23
Chinese Yellow 26
Common Mime 20
Common Mormon 21
Common Rose 18
Great Mormon 22
Lime 26
Paris Peacock 24
Red Helen 25
Southern Chinese Peacock 24
Spangle 23
Tawny Mime 20
Swift, Bevan's 54
   Colon 60
   Conjoined 58
   Contiguous 59
   Continental 52
   Dark 60
   Formosan 53
   Great 58
   Paintbrush 59
Swordtail, Five-bar 16
Symbrenthia lilaea 120

Tagiades litigiosa 33
   menaka 33
Tajuria cippus 155
   maculata 156
Tanaecia whiteheadi
   (*Euthalia niepelti*) 111
Taraka hamada 129
Taractrocera ceramas 49
   maevius 49
Telchinia (*Acraea*)
   issoria 93
Telicota bambusae 48
   besta 47
   colon 48
   ohara 46

Thoressa monastyrskyi 39
Three-Ring, Small 90
Tiger Butterfly, Blue 74
   Ceylon Blue Glassy 73
   Chestnut 76
   Chocolate 76
   Common 72
   Dark Blue 75
   Glassy 75
   Plain 72
Tirumala limniace 74
   septentrionis 75
Tit, Fluffy 154
Treebrown, Bamboo 91
   Banded 91
   Common 92
Troides aeacus 18
   helena 18

Udara albocaerulea 144
   dilecta 144
Udaspes folus 43

Vanessa cardui 119
   indica 120

Windmill, Chinese 18

Ypthima baldus 88
   imitans 90
   lisandra 89
   norma 90
   praenubila 89

Zeltus amasa 154
Zemeros flegyas 126
Zizeeria karsandra 148
Zizina otis 149
Zizula hylax 149
Zographetus satwa 40